THE RELATION OF THOMAS JEFFERSON
TO AMERICAN FOREIGN POLICY
1783-1793

SERIES XLV   No. 2

JOHNS HOPKINS UNIVERSITY STUDIES

IN

HISTORICAL AND POLITICAL SCIENCE

Under the Direction of the

Departments of History, Political Economy, and
Political Science

———

THE RELATION OF THOMAS JEFFERSON TO AMERICAN FOREIGN POLICY 1783-1793

BY

WILLIAM KIRK WOOLERY, PH. D.

Head of Department of History, Bethany College

———

BALTIMORE
THE JOHNS HOPKINS PRESS
1927

Republished by
Scholarly Press, Inc., 22929 Industrial Drive East
St. Clair Shores, Michigan 48080

TO THE MEMORY OF
MY MOTHER

PREFACE

The limits of the period in which the foreign policy of the United States was first evolved and put into practice may be marked off by the Declaration of Independence and Jay's Treaty of 1794. It was within this stretch of years that the nation emerged and took its place among the powers of the world, albeit not that " separate and equal station " to which the ambitious framers of the Declaration aspired. Propitious as the circumstances were at the time of the introduction of this new member into the international family, the changes of the age which brought on a still greater revolution in France, forced quick and significant decisions on the part of the United States in its relations with the rest of the world, thus necessitating the enunciation of fundamental rules for controlling its foreign policy. With the three countries of Europe whose colonizing efforts of preceding centuries had laid the basis of American development, the United States struggled to reach understandings which would promote the realization of unhampered independence as well as provide rules for amicable intercourse.

Only a decade, however, separated the treaty of peace which assured the independence of the United States from the beginning of the war between the French Republic and monarchical Europe. That period tested severely the outcome of the American Revolution; it verified the unwelcome fact that although political independence was generally recognized, yet the French alliance and the French and Dutch debts remained to restrain that freedom; that while commercial independence was an object of highest importance, in fact the chief concern after 1783, nowhere did the United States receive such treatment as she sought; that even though the boundaries were established for the most part by treaty definition and with appreciation of the just claims of Spain and Great Britain, yet the integrity of the territory in the West was not respected by either power. Thus the obligations

assumed by the United States and by the European powers
concerned in the treaties by which American affairs were settled in 1782-1783 furnished but a single definite guide for
the conduct of future relations between the United States and
the other states participating in the war, and that was that
the United States should retain her political independence.

Not thoroughly respected at home, it was impossible to be
so abroad. In the years after 1783 the new state had to determine the basis for its commercial relations, protect its
trade by treaties, relieve its citizens from the menace of Barbary pirates, adjust claims and debts,—in general to achieve
a satisfactory position among the nations. And this achievement was a serious proposition to a government which was
but poorly adapted to overcome even the ordinary difficulties
of domestic concerns. For the solution Thomas Jefferson
was largely responsible. As minister to France and as Secretary of State, he attacked every problem of American diplomacy, and the systems and principles he followed were, in
practically every case, ultimately followed by the United
States. It is the purpose of this study to investigate the chief
problems and the reasoning Jefferson applied to them, in the
period 1783-1793.

W. K. W.

CONTENTS

			PAGE
Preface			vii
Chapter	I.	Post-war Commercial Commissions...	1
Chapter	II.	Negotiations with the Barbary Pirates	20
Chapter	III.	French-American Commerce	40
Chapter	IV.	The Consular Convention of 1788....	58
Chapter	V.	Treaties Obstructed	66
Chapter	VI.	British and French Treaties	85
Chapter	VII.	Neutrality	103
Bibliography			123

THE RELATION OF THOMAS JEFFERSON TO AMERICAN FOREIGN POLICY, 1783-1793

CHAPTER I

The Post-War Commercial Commissions

A defensive foreign policy is a mark of maturity in national existence. Exclusiveness in commerce colors the history of modern colonization and exhibits in the few exceptions as well as in the usual practice a determination to maintain the existing system. If a settled policy may be said to have existed at one time more than at another, the decade preceding the outbreak of the French Revolution witnessed it. The principles of British commercial regulations dominated the commercial world, for despite the appearance of radicalism in the First Armed Neutrality and the departures from her ancient maritime code made by France in her two American treaties, Great Britain held inexorably to the principles of her old and successful maritime regulations, and, where Great Britain led, others followed. As Admiral Mahan has said: "Nor was there in the thought of the age, external to Great Britain, any corrective of the impressions which dominated her commercial policy."[1] In fact, the important colonial powers were thoroughly animated by the spirit of the English Navigation Acts, acting upon the same principles and toward the same goal of commercial monopoly.

This unpromising aspect of European tendencies was recognized by Americans on both sides of the Atlantic, although it was not clearly seen in Congress that the position of the nation in regard to commercial standing after the preliminary treaty of 1782 was much the same as its political status after the Declaration of Independence. But among the commis-

---

[1] A. T. Mahan, Sea Power in its Relations to the War of 1812, p. 27.

1

sioners of the United States in Europe considerable anxiety was felt over the future of treaty relations between their country and those powers with which no agreements had been obtained. John Adams, in particular, was disturbed by the negligence of Congress in failing to furnish full powers to some of the envoys, probably himself especially,[2] to conclude a commercial treaty with Great Britain. On May 24, 1783, he wrote Livingston: " It is much to be wished that the definitive treaty of peace and a permanent treaty of commerce could be signed at the same time. This, however, seems now to be impossible." [3]

Yet at this very time, David Hartley, who had been a chief instrument in promoting peace between the two countries, gave assurances that any of the American agents would be received in London on the same footing as the minister of any other independent power.[4] Adams did not know that Congress had acted, at the beginning of the same month,[5] on his earlier letters, and had ordered a commission to be made out to the three commissioners, or any of them, to undertake a permanent treaty of commerce and to arrange for the intervening period by a provisional convention to continue in force for not more than a year. But no such commission was sent; nor did the secretary for foreign affairs, Robert Livingston, prepare a plan and instructions for treaties with other nations of Europe, since he resigned shortly after this duty was laid upon him.[6] Hence the definitive treaty with Great Britain was signed without any disposition of commercial questions except, of course, in so far as the treaty of 1783 was in itself commercial.

---

[2] The commission and instructions for negotiating a treaty of commerce with Great Britain, given to Adams by Congress September 29, 1779, were revoked July 12, 1781 (Secret Journals of Congress, Foreign Affairs, vol. ii, p. 463; Wharton, Diplomatic Correspondence of the American Revolution, vol. iv, p. 849).

[3] Life and Works of John Adams, ed. by Adams, vol. viii, p. 60.

[4] Ibid. Hartley, however, was not entirely in the confidence of his own government (Channing, History of the United States, vol. iii, p. 353.

[5] Sec. Jour., vol. iii, p. 340.

[6] The resolution ordering it was passed May 1. Livingston resigned June 4 (Journals of the Continental Congress, vol. xxiv, p. 382).

But during the summer of that year, letters from the ministers in Paris kept reminding Congress that vigorous action speaks a universal language; that feebleness in our foreign policy was encouraging Great Britain to reimpose on the United States, just as in colonial days, the Navigation Acts, with the consequence of legislating [7] American shipping out of the British West Indies, and of restraining the importation of commodities from the United States into England to British bottoms or to those of the state which produced the articles.[8] With the probability of similar exclusion by France the commerce of the United States would be seriously handicapped, in fact, that part of it which nature had made the most important, the West Indian trade, would be practically lost.

So much importuned, Congress finally felt constrained to take action, appointing a committee whose report, September 29, suggested as a remedy a recommendation to the States; and an equally impotent second proposal for two special committees to consider general commercial and political arrangements for our foreign connections.[9] Of these, one committee did prepare a draft of instructions to the American ministers at Versailles, to which Congress gave its approval on October 29. It covered the points raised by previous discussions; but it was devoid of principles for the guidance of American envoys in "encouraging the dispositions of the other commercial powers in Europe for entering into treaties of amity and commerce with these United States," [10] merely restating the former principles that treaties should be made on the basis of perfect equality and reciprocity, with terms not inconsistent with any previous treaties of the United States,

---

[7] Sec. Jour., vol. iii, p. 398; H. C. Bell, " Trade Relations between the British West Indies and North America, 1783-1793," in English Historical Review, July, 1916, p. 435.

[8] The Life and Writings of Benjamin Franklin, ed. by Smyth, vol. ix, pp. 30, 49, 59, 96; Adams, Works, vol. viii, pp. 398-400.

[9] The difference of opinion in Congress had been over whether the United States should energetically seek favors abroad by a group of commissioners, or employ a central-executive system of diplomacy and endeavor to treat as a full equal.

[10] Sec. Jour., vol. iii, p. 412.

and limited to a term of fifteen years. As for the Armed Neutrality, the United States did not wish " to become a party to a confederacy which may hereafter too far complicate the interests of the United States with the politicks of Europe " ; [11] and, while approving the principles of that organization, instructions were given to ministers in Europe not to further American admission or participation in it.[12]

This was the eventual disposition of rules for foreign connections during the session of the Third Congress. A sense that it was insufficient seems to have remained with the members. Boudinot, retiring president, wrote to Adams, November 1, to acknowledge his letters of June and July, saying: " Nothing is done in consequence of these letters but what is contained in the instructions enclosed in my official letter by this opportunity to the commissioners jointly." [13] Moreover the reception of these new advices by the persons to whom they were directed was not enthusiastic. Franklin's reply pointed out the omission of instructions on the Danish and Portuguese treaties, the inadvisability of making advances to other powers when no relations had been established, and above all the failure to send the commission for a commercial treaty with England, a matter of deep concern to Adams and a puzzling irritation to Franklin.[14]

To the new Congress, called to assemble on November 3, there was thus left a number of problems connected with foreign affairs. The definitive treaty had been received too late to be acted on by the Third Congress; some definite establishment was needed for conducting the nation's relations with other countries, both in respect to principles of legisla-

[11] Ibid., p. 415.

[12] Dana's opinion that the Tsarina Catherine did not want any kind of political connection with the United States undoubtedly held true for the Armed Neutrality after the war as well as during it (cf. Wharton, vol. v, p. 223).

[13] Adams, Works, vol. viii, p. 153. He did, however, in a letter of the same date to the commissioners, say officially that these instructions had undergone " the most mature deliberation and fullest discussion in Congress " (Wharton, vol. vi, p. 720).

[14] Adams, Works, vol. viii, p. 164; Franklin, Writings, vol. ix, p. 130 ff.

tion and in an executive department with a permanent secretary at its head. But Congress met at New York on the appointed day only to adjourn the next. A new location, Annapolis, was chosen and the date set forward to the twenty-sixth of the month. On the latter date a lack of representation prevented the opening of the session, and for almost three weeks the punctual members paid the penalty for their virtue by waiting in idleness and in speculating on the prospects of having in attendance the required number of States to ratify the treaty.[15]

Among these early arrivals was Thomas Jefferson, head of the Virginia delegation; to him fell the duty of examining and reporting the form of ratification; and at the same time he was made chairman of a committee to take under consideration the letter of September 10 from the ministers at Paris. A committee on unfinished business had, directly upon the meeting of Congress at Annapolis, classified the matters which would claim the attention of Congress, under five headings, and in the first had put the most important items, including the ratification of the definitive treaty and the "civil arrangements foreign and domestic." These required the assent of nine States. On December 16, a report on the treaty was submitted, recommending ratification and proper legislation by the States for restitution of confiscated British property to bona fide owners, while resolutions introduced into Congress at about the same time held the American negotiators to "require with firmness and decision" satisfaction for slaves and other property carried away by the British, "in violation of the preliminary and definitive articles of peace";[16] and to this Jefferson would have added that any demand for interest on debts owed to British creditors, accumulating during the war period, was "highly inequitable and unjust."[17]

[15] The Writings of Thomas Jefferson, ed. by Ford, Federal Edition, vol. iv, pp. 177, 180.
[16] Jefferson, Writings, vol. iv, p. 189.
[17] The Jefferson Manuscripts, December, 1783, Library of Congress. Hereafter referred to as J. MSS.

After a week's silence on this subject,—the period when Washington " had his last audience of Congress, laid down his connection and bid a final adieu to them and to all public life,"—Jefferson gave vent to his emotion over the spectacle of the highest legislative body in the nation rendered impotent by the indifference of almost half of the States. His correspondence at this time is filled with his anxiety about the situation.[18] Only a little more than two months remained before ratifications had to be exchanged. On December 27, he presented a document of some length, laboring to explain why a Congress of but seven States could not constitutionally ratify this or any other treaty, apparently leaving a loop-hole in the expression " without proper explanations," but at the same time stating that, since sixty-seven days remained and the measures adopted to bring in representatives from the recreant States would presumably be effective, they should risk waiting until nine States had assented to the treaty, and, if late, urge the minor importance of a few days' delay.[19] However, the necessary number was represented early in 1784, and on January 14 the final ratification was adopted in the form reported by Jefferson's committee.[20]

When the American ministers at Paris sent the draft of the definitive treaty to Congress, September 10, 1783, they enclosed a report of the general attitude that prevailed among the European powers on the commercial connections they might make with the United States. Just what final conclusion Great Britain would reach on this head was not clear. David Hartley had consistently represented the desires and intentions of his government as highly favorable to the initiation of negotiations;[21] but when at last the American plenipotentiaries signified that Congress had empowered them to undertake such a treaty, the ministry at London suddenly

[18] Ibid., Dec., 1783-Jan., 1784.
[19] Jefferson, Writings, vol. iv, p. 204; Franklin, Writings, vol. ix, p. 176; The Diplomatic Correspondence of the United States, 1783-1789, vol. ii, p. 21.
[20] Sec. Jour., vol. iii, p. 433.
[21] Franklin, Writings, vol. ix, pp. 26, 87, 109.

assumed that air of indifference and inscrutable silence which was shown for almost a decade afterwards.

In this letter to Congress there is an indication of the reason for the change in policy, at least the cause that Franklin and Adams believed responsible. They were awaiting instructions on a proposition Hartley had made early in the summer; these orders, however, did not reach them by the expected vessel. The letter continues: " But at that time information arrived from America that our ports were all opened to British vessels. Mr. Hartley thereupon did not think himself at liberty to proceed until after he should communicate that intelligence to his court and receive their further instructions. These further instructions never came; and thus our endeavors as to commercial regulations proved fruitless." [22]

On the other hand, with continental Europe, treaties of commerce were feasible at this time, but Congress had not set itself to the business. Worse still, the commissioners were in the dark as to the intentions of that body, so that when they received intimations of the good disposition of a prince toward the United States they were legally powerless to clinch the advantage with a definite proposition.[23] However broadly they viewed their powers and obligations, they felt that restrictions had been set to their activities by the lack of both specific commissions and embracing instructions. Their communications to America, both official and private, during the year 1783 laid unmistakable emphasis on this failure of Congress, while at the same time pointing out the need of meeting the advances of Portugal, Prussia, Morocco, and the Italian States, and of approaching Spain by a separate minister.[24] This information, and particularly the official communication

[22] Wharton, vol. vi, p. 688. Jefferson also accepted this as the cause of suspension of negotiations for a commercial treaty (Writings, vol. iv, p. 184; H. C. Bell, " Trade Relations Between the British West Indies and North America," in English Historical Review, July, 1916, p. 433).

[23] Franklin, Writings, vol. ix, pp. 29, 50, 110.

[24] Wharton, vol. vi, pp. 294-743, passim; Adams, Works, vol. viii, pp. 74, 85, 95, 104, 150; Franklin, Writings, vol. ix, pp. 49, 59, 97, 129.

of September 10, brought about a reconsideration of the entire foreign establishment. Without repudiating the action of October 29, Jefferson led Congress to lay a foundation for relations with other nations that was comprehensive, logical, and expedient. It borrowed important principles from the experience of the Revolution but introduced some rules of procedure new to American practice.[25]

Foreign affairs were first taken up on December 20 in a "Report on Letters from the Ministers in Paris," [26] but attention was diverted to Washington's retirement and then to the treaty of peace, so that it was late in March before deliberation was begun on the propositions made in the report. Mercer, member of the Virginia delegation, proposed that all negotiations for European treaties should be conducted in the United States and the results laid before the States for their concurrence, to which Jefferson answered by a set of " resolves," showing the futility of expecting the nations of the Old World, " antient and established as they are," to come soliciting from a new nation, and demonstrating the unconstitutionality of the plan in so far as it necessitated state rather than national sanction for the conclusion of treaties.[27] On this point his views prevailed in Congress and, beyond some inconsequential debates over salaries of ministers, no difference of opinion was found on the subject. On May 7, 1784, Jay was elected Secretary for Foreign Affairs, Jeffer-

[25] Compare the provisions of the French, Swedish, and Dutch treaties of 1778-1783 with these new instructions on (1) Removal of restraints from markets and the carrying trade between the United States and the American possessions of European powers; (2) On the carrying of own produce in own vessels; (3) On abolition of privateering, so far as innocent commerce was concerned; (4) On doing away with uncompensated confiscation of private property under the name of contraband; and (5) On abrogating disqualification of land inheritance because of alienage. The Jefferson Manuscripts have notes on the instructions in Jefferson's writing, and rough drafts are placed with the letters of December, 1783. There is a fair copy of the instructions under date of May 7, 1784. The similarity of these propositions and the terms of the Prussian treaty of 1785 provides interesting speculation as to whether Jefferson received any suggestions from Franklin.
[26] Jefferson, Writings, vol. iv, p. 189. Not in Sec. Jour.
[27] Ibid., pp. 274, 353; Sec. Jour., vol. iii, p. 483.

son was made minister plenipotentiary to aid Franklin and Adams in negotiating treaties of commerce, and Jefferson's report of the preceding December 20 was adopted as the basis upon which these treaties were to be concluded.

The instructions begin by naming the commercial powers of Europe with which it would be advantageous to have treaties,—Russia, the Empire, Prussia, Denmark, Saxony, Hamburg, Great Britain, Spain, Portugal, Genoa, Tuscany, Rome, Naples, Venice, Sardinia, and Turkey,—all the important nations that were not then in treaty relation with the United States. Then certain principles were laid down for " careful stipulation " in the treaty scheme, arranged in order of importance, with the essential and mandatory ideas contained in the first three sections.

The first was the proviso that in general commercial relations the right of each party to transport its own exports and imports in its own vessels should be unhindered, and that in respect to duties the basis should be that of the most favored nation.[28] The proclamations made in England less than a year before this would have prevented a convention between the two countries on any such ground as this, and undoubtedly the realization of both the English and the French post-bellum commercial systems colored the second article of the instructions.[29] This concerned the trade between the United States and the American possessions of European states, and proposed that this branch be put on the footing of direct and similar intercourse; or, if such privileges should be refused, then that direct trade be carried on between the United States and certain free ports in those possessions; and, as a final alternative, if neither of the other plans proved acceptable, that " these " states should export their produce in their own vessels to such possessions directly, and they should export in like manner to the United States.[30] There

---

[28] Jefferson to Adams, July 31, 1785, J. MSS.
[29] Above, page 3.
[30] Jefferson believed that if we failed to get such treatment then, with European nations so disposed, we would lose an advantage not easily regained (J. MSS., Dec., 1783).

was evidently no expectation that the trade between the colonies and Europe would be opened to any carriers but those of the mother country; but any of the three suggested plans, if adopted, would have removed for the United States the worst restrictions of the navigation laws and the colonial monopolies maintained by Great Britain and her imitators.

The next point in the instructions answered, or assumed to answer, those foreign critics who believed that the American nation was about to break up and who cited as proof the cases of conflicting laws and the lack of response of both the States and the people to the central government. To these detractors it was stated that in the making of treaties and in disposing of cases arising under them, the United States was to be considered "as one nation, upon the principles of the federal constitution." [31]

With these indispensable requisites cared for, the instructions take up the treatment of the persons and property of alien enemies in case of war between the United States and the other contracting party. Merchants were to be allowed nine months to settle their affairs and then were to be unmolested if they wished to leave the country; but if they preferred to remain and pursue their business, "exchanging the products of different places, and thereby rendering the necessaries, conveniences, and comforts of human life more easy to obtain," they were to be free to do so. Peaceable artisans, unarmed and living in unfortified places, were to follow their occupations without other disturbance than being obliged to furnish such of their goods as were needed by the armed forces of the land, and this only for a reasonable price. As for property at sea, neither side was to commission privateers to destroy private shipping.

The next article deals with the commerce of one party as neutral in a war which involved the other. The regulation of contraband should not be determined so as to cause confiscation or loss of property to individuals, although ships carrying such goods might be detained and the goods themselves taken for use of the captors if compensation were made to the owners. As for non-contraband goods, the rule of free ships free goods should prevail, and in endeavoring to determine the character of the goods, an unwarranted detention of an innocent merchant-man by a belligerent vessel would provide cause for damages. This assertion has something of the spirit of the rules which the First Armed Neutrality sought to introduce.[32] The definition of a blockade likewise imitates the pronouncement of that confederation, both falling back on an old rule of the law of nations: " To ascertain what shall constitute the blockade of any place or port, it shall be understood to be in such predicament when the assailing power shall have taken such a station as to expose to imminent danger any ship or ships, that would attempt to sail in or out of the said port." [33]

No stipulation was admissible that would grant aliens the right to hold real property in the states since their laws and policy were opposed to it. But if at the death of a citizen of either contracting party his real estate would legally descend to a citizen or subject of the other except for the disqualification of alienage, then such heir should be allowed to sell the property and withdraw the proceeds.

Treaties made under these regulations were limited to a life of ten years, although in freeing the negotiators from too rigid adherence to the provisions as set forth in these instructions, an allowance was made for exceptional cases in which the term might be extended to fifteen years; and in other details, or even in basic principles, where greater benefits could be secured to the United States by a different plan, the ministers were permitted to depart from the regulations. But that such latitude would not be used is intimated when a further step was taken by suggesting that supplementary treaties with France, the Netherlands, and Sweden be sought in order to " bring the treaties we have entered into with them as nearly as may be to the principles of those now

---

[32] J. B. Scott, The Armed Neutralities of 1780 and 1800, p. 274.
[33] Sec. Jour., vol. iii, p. 487; Jefferson, Writings, vol. iv, p. 193.

directed." This, however, was made to depend on the dispositions of those powers.

With the group of states on the north coast of Africa, the Barbary States, a different treatment was necessary and a separate grant of power for that purpose was made, although it was given to the charge of the same persons. The advances already made by the Emperor of Morocco were to be met, apology for American delay proffered, and readiness to proceed to a treaty with him explained. The only principle laid down for these treaties, aside from the minimum term of ten years, was acquiescence in that vicious practice of European nations of paying tribute for protection to their commerce. The American ministers were told that "as to the expenses of his Minister, they do therein what is for the honor and interest of the United States." [34]

The duties implied in this new establishment of diplomacy were place upon Franklin, Adams, and Jefferson, their commissions running for two years and their place of residence at the court of his most Christian Majesty where it was expected they would most readily make contact with the powers of Europe through the various ambassadors at Versailles, as well as receive the advice of Vergennes. Jefferson did not believe the business of getting commercial treaties with European states would be a difficult task. As he wrote to Madison: "The plan of Foreign Affairs likely to take place is to commission Adams, Franklin & Jay to conclude treaties with the several European powers, and then to return, leaving the field to subordinate characters." [35]

Congress adopted these instructions in the words used by Jefferson in writing the committee's report, and this is as far as they dealt with the matter. [36] His view that there should be no trade where there was no treaty did not suffice to command the waves of the economic sea. While his system was

[34] In the original there was added: "and conformable to the practice of other nations"; these words were scratched out (J. MSS., Dec. 20, 1783).
[35] Writings, vol. iv, p. 241, February 20, 1784.
[36] Sec. Jour., vol. iii, pp. 484, 493; J. MSS., Dec. 20, 1783.

but a new rendition of former principles, he was about to assume the duty of vindicating them by becoming chief diplomatic officer of the United States, first for five years as minister to France, and then for four more as Secretary of State.

Shortly after Congress had concluded this important piece of legislation and while his commission was being prepared, Jefferson left Annapolis for Philadelphia. After several weeks there, he proceeded slowly on through New York and the New England States, investigating carefully the condition of northern industries and acquiring the viewpoint of that section on commerce and manufacturing. From Boston he took passage, July 5, on the *Ceres,* and by August 6 was in Paris, being but nineteen days from land to land. After a few days' rest, he went to Passy to confer with Franklin on the business their commissions imposed on them, meanwhile writing to Adams to inform him of his new appointment and requesting him to come to Paris.[37] Among the commissions were three relating to France, Sweden, and the Netherlands, for, although treaties had already been signed with these countries, it was believed that amendments were desirable, and, moreover, without being accredited to France in some official capacity, both Jefferson and Adams would be without diplomatic status there, subject to the civil law.[38] The other commissions were for the proposed commercial treaties with some twenty powers. As Franklin observed, " We are not likely to eat the bread of idleness; and that we may not surfeit by eating too much, our masters have diminished our allowance." [39]

The three ministers began their work in a meeting at Passy, August 30, when they decided to meet every day until their objects had been " put as far as may be, into the best train of execution." This resolution was more nobly made than kept; but it is certain that they attacked the courts of Europe

---

[37] Memoirs, ed. by T. J. Randolph, vol. i, p. 49.
[38] Writings, vol. iv, p. 359; Jefferson to Monroe, June 18, 1784, J. MSS.
[39] Franklin, Writings, vol. ix, p. 250.

with remarkable ardor and a degree of success not to be expected from a nation so recently a group of rebellious colonies.[40]   Letters were addressed to the representatives of Denmark, Great Britain, Portugal, Spain, Russia, Saxony, Sicily, Sardinia, the Pope, Venice, Tuscany, Prussia, the Empire, Sweden, Genoa, and France, proposing either new or supplementary treaties, and answers were received from most of these courts.   But here the advances stopped; in fact actual negotiations were undertaken with but few of the states named since their results would, in the opinion of the ministers, be of doubtful outcome, hinging almost entirely on the relations which might be established with the more influential powers on the Atlantic coast.   Moreover, the proposal which Franklin had made to Hartley during the negotiations of the preceding year was now, with the approval of his colleagues, inserted into the tentative form suggested to such nations as were disposed to treat with the United States.[41]   This proposal was the abolition of privateering, refused by England; and with it were connected in the plan, the principle of " free ships free goods "; a provision to prevent molestation of peaceful, unarmed aliens in time of war; abandonment of the practice of making contraband of war an excuse for confiscating vessels; and regulations for the humane treatment of prisoners of war.

To these rather unusual propositions only one nation in Europe made serious counter-proposals, and that one,— Prussia,—an inland country with whom commercial relations were not highly desirable, at best.   But before considering the negotiations which resulted in the remarkable treaty of 1785, we find a more pertinent subject thrust on our attention. This is the subject of the most favored nation principle as applied to the entire extent of treaties to which the United States had bound herself, or was to bind herself.

A letter from Monroe to Jefferson of July 20, 1784, contained this very query.[42]   What, he inquired, are the possi-

---

[40] Dip. Cor., vol. ii, pp. 196, 198, 202, 205-239
[41] Ibid., p. 224; Memoirs, vol. ii, p. 50.
[42] The Writings of James Monroe, ed. by Hamilton, vol. i, p. 36.

bili‌‌es under this plan of making regulations that will induce
reciprocal advantages from other nations? Thus, Virginia
had just enacted a law whose operation was suspended for two
years, by which foreign vessels were to be restricted to one
port on each river in the State. But, he continued, suppose
Spain should remove or lighten the duties on American commerce and we should try to reciprocate. " Can we and is it
consistent with the usage of nations to give her reciprocal
advantages here, the treaties between us and each power being,
as that with France, on the principle of the right of the
' most favored nation ' "? His question, he averred, was
directed more toward information on actual international
practice than on the "usual import of the words." To this
Jefferson answered, December 10, that he did not know of
any investigation of the extent of the clause giving most
favored nations rights; but reasoning from the words themselves, as used to express the idea that a privilege granted to
any nation immediately became common, freely where freely
given, or upon paying the same compensation, when any
compensation was demanded,—he did not doubt that if any
nation would admit our goods free of duty in consideration
of our doing the same, another nation could not claim exemption in our ports without yielding us the same right in
theirs.[43]

Even free entry, or what purported to be free entry, was
not, however, a solution for equitable commercial arrangements so long as governments encouraged monopolies. France
granted several " free " ports to Americans but at the same
time controlled the entry of goods by subjecting them to the
monopolistic disposition of the Farmers General, a regulation
which was little short of exclusion, inasmuch as it permitted
imports to reach the market only under the heaviest burdens
and in restricted quantities.[44] The same artificial conditions
were created in Portugal by the administration of the corn
market where free entry for American flour was offset by

---

[43] Writings, vol. iv, p. 385.
[44] Letter from Joseph Wharton to Charles Thompson, Oct. 26, 1784,
J. MSS.

restriction of sales to such "dribbling lots" as to dispose of scarcely a cargo in a year; and in the London tobacco market, which then fixed the price for the world, prices were manufactured through monopolization by a few brokers who controlled distribution and manipulated the public auctions.[45]

But in the latter case it was a matter of price and not of admission into England; a treaty could neither raise the price nor prevent an over-supply in the market. More than anything else this showed that the most favored nation principle worked to the disadvantage of that nation whose system was most liberal; it was quite different from the principle of reciprocity, and was so recognized by Jay when he, as secretary for foreign affairs, reported on the plan of a treaty of commerce proposed for Prussia and the United States. With curious disregard for the instructions of May 7, he informed Congress that a system should be adopted for the regulation of trade before treaties were made rather than afterwards; that the most favored nation policy was not expedient, for several reasons.

In the first place, European nations were firmly settled in their trade systems whereas the United States was a beginner; besides, there was a distinction between granting favors to a country "merely European" and one "partly European and partly American"; interchanged advantages might be "exactly similar in kind, and yet very different in value"; and, finally, what might be granted *freely* to one nation might not be granted at all to another, and "as our trade is at present free to all, we have few *favors* to grant to any; whereas, their trade being charged with various duties and restrictions, they need only relax to have favors to grant." [46] To this opinion Jay held, although not so rigidly but that he finally recommended the ratification of the treaty a year

---

[45] Letter from "N. J." to Jefferson, July 12, 1784, J. MSS. This letter is not listed in the Calendar of Jefferson Correspondence, in Jefferson's letter index, nor in the index books of the Department of Foreign Affairs. Also printed letter of Henry Martin, Oct. 5, J. MSS.

[46] Dip. Cor., vol. ii, pp. 232-235. For another argument against the most favored nation plan, see a letter from Elbridge Gerry to Jefferson, Feb. 25, 1785, J. MSS.

later. On the other hand, Jefferson adhered to the view he originally expressed in Congress, and on this Franklin and Adams agreed with him. On one phase, however, Jay and Jefferson were in accord. That was in respect to differentiating between powers holding American colonial possessions and those that did not. Writing to Monroe, to whom he usually expressed himself fully, Jefferson went on to expound his ideas on principles. "The effecting treaties with the powers holding positions in the West Indies, I consider as the important part of our business. It is not of great consequence whether the others treat or not. Perhaps trade may go on with them well enough without. But Britain, Spain, Portugal, France are consequent, and Holland, Denmark, Sweden may be of service too." [47]

With the experience of several more months, and after his appointment as minister to France, he "hazarded" some further thoughts on treaty policy in another letter to Monroe, though acknowledging that he was prepared to relinquish them "chearfully" if Congress should adopt others. He found that Congress was given power by the Articles of Confederation to assume jurisdiction over the commerce of the States only through its treaty-making privilege, and was limited in the exercise of that jurisdiction to the objects included within the scope of the treaties. The Articles restrained the Confederation in the use of this power in two essentials: First, no treaty might interfere with the right of the States to levy "such duties on foreigners as their own people are subject to"; and secondly, it should not prevent the States from prohibiting the exportation or importation of "any particular species of goods." But aside from these restrictions, the Confederation was entrusted with the formation of a system of commerce, by means of treaties, and, in Jefferson's opinion, it was highly expedient to contract such relations with all trading nations on the most favored nation plan if by so doing the central government could "put an

[47] February, 1785. The date of the month is not given (Writings, vol. iv, p. 395).

end to the right of individual states acting by fits and starts
to interrupt our commerce or to embroil us with any nation."

As to the more fundamental factors, from the diplomatic
viewpoint, of deciding the nature of a treaty, he showed three
different plans. First, that of trade entirely free from duties;
secondly, of duties equalized to charges of the other party;
and thirdly, the most favored nation duties. Free trade he
rejected because European systems were differently organized
and so rigidly fixed as to preclude its adoption; equalization
of import charges he considered impossible both in determination and in execution, likely to "end in anything sooner
than equality"; the last plan, then, remained, but he pointed
out the simplicity of operation under this scheme,—it allowed
general regulation while giving security against discrimination
or partiality, was easily comprehended, and was in force. He
admitted that a serious obstacle existed in the fact that trade
with the West Indies was denied to the United States, and
the only price left to exchange for it was admission of the
commerce of the mother country into the ports of the United
States, on the basis of native citizen rights,—" and to those
who refuse . . . we must refuse our commerce or load theirs
by odious discriminations in our ports." [48] . . . " The mis-
fortune is that with this country [France] we gave this price
for their aid in the war, and we have now nothing more to
offer. She being withdrawn from the competition leaves
Great Britain much more at liberty to hold out against us.
This is the difficult part of the business of treaty, and I own
it does not hold out the most flattering prospect." [49]

While Jefferson was thus evolving his principles for diplomacy in general, the treaty with Prussia was nearing com-
pletion. The project submitted by the three ministers to the
Prussian Minister at the Hague, Baron de Thulemeir, contained two unusual stipulations. The first was intended to
abolish contraband so far as it involved loss of property to

---

[48] This, of course, could not have been done under a most favored
nation treaty, but Jefferson had Great Britain in mind.
[49] Writings, vol. iv, p. 424.

individuals; the second would prevent the seizure of private property on land merely because of enemy ownership and not because of the probability of hostile acts by the owners.[50] Since Prussia did not maintain war vessels, she had no objection to binding herself to these articles, and while Franklin was leaving France the final details were being cared for by Jefferson. His secretary, William Short, was sent to the Hague to act with Charles Dumas in the final ceremonies. Concluded September 10, 1785, the treaty was referred to Congress where it was ratified after a short debate, having suffered no damage from Jay's futile criticism, and in October of 1786 ratifications were exchanged at the Hague.

The importance of this treaty is that it was symptomatic. It was idealistic, and yet an idealism that the New World felt might be made practicable. The democracy which had germinated in the United States and grown to be one of its peculiar and distinctive characteristics, had un-Europeanized its diplomacy in this treaty. It had placed this country in such a position among the nations as to make possible the preservation of an original liberalism and a unique influence on international obligations.

---

[50] Dip. Cor., vol. ii, pp. 219-239; J. S. Williams, The Permanent Influence of Thomas Jefferson on American Institutions, p. 109; Syngman Rhee, Neutrality as Influenced by the United States, p. 23; French Transcripts, Affaires Etrangères, Correspondance Politique, Etats-Unis, vol. xxxi, No. 51. Article XIII of the treaty was repeated in the Prussian treaties of 1799 and 1823; see James Brown Scott's Treaties between the United States and Prussia, pp. 160-183, for the case of the *William P. Frye* involving this matter.

CHAPTER II

NEGOTIATIONS WITH THE BARBARY PIRATES

Robert Montgomery, the first merchant from the United States to establish a business in Spain, anticipated the official representatives in communicating to the Emperor of Morocco the desire of the United States to begin negotiations for a treaty. This forwardness was resented by Franklin, who doubted the wisdom of beginning to buy off the Barbary states until American trade in the Mediterranean became more important. On the other hand, Thomas Barclay, Consul-General of the United States in France, considered it as important as any American business in Europe.

This phase of the instructions of May 7 was postponed while the Prussian treaty was in process and until the three envoys could learn what method of procedure promised greatest probability of success. Their alternatives, they believed, would eventually be presents or war. Adams favored presents even though he could not convince himself that it was the honorable, or even the expedient, course. His reasoning was not particularly acute; affirming in one breath that the United States could not afford to wage such a war, he admitted in the next that he did not know where money for presents could be found.[1] Jefferson inclined toward war,—an attitude of considerable importance in view of its subsequent application. He took pains to learn the sums given by the nations of Europe to purchase peace, but without much success, guessing that it would amount to as much as three hundred thousand dollars. "Surely," he said, "our people will not give this. Would it not be better to offer them an equal treaty? If they refuse, why not go to war with them? . . . We ought to begin a naval power, if we mean to carry our own commerce. . . . I am of opinion Paul Jones with half a dozen frigates would totally destroy their commerce; not by attempting bombard-

---

[1] Adams, Works, vol. viii, p. 217.

ments as the Mediterranean states do wherein they act against the whole Barbary force brought to a point, but by constant cruizing and cutting them to pieces by piecemeal." [2]

The necessity of acting promptly was demonstrated by the news of the capture by the Moroccans of the American brig *Betsy,* on October 11, 1784. This decided the envoys at Paris to apply, officially, to Vergennes for advice and assistance.[3] The result of this appeal was to remove American diplomacy another degree from French guidance and to set it upon its own feet, for Vergennes had only meagre advice and evaded the main question by referring them to M. de Sartine and M. de Castries, in whose departments rather than in his the matter belonged. Their answers were to the effect that if the United States intended to make treaties with Barbary, France could and would help; that if she wished only to make her flag respected, it could not be done, considering the deceit of the pirates; but they felt that Congress was informed on presents and prices for peace, and that an ambassadorial agent should be sent to Morocco. Recent developments had justified the opinion of these ministers as to the information the United States possessed on the tribute paid by European nations. The fifth report of the envoys in France, made April 13, 1785, includes items on the number of captives at Algiers, the price for peace, the amounts usually paid by the Christian powers, and other interesting facts which had been furnished to them by Lafayette, without, however, any pretense at exactness.[4]

Congress felt that the authority given to its envoys in Europe to treat with the pirate states would be sufficient to create proper relations in that direction, and to give security to American commerce with southern Europe.[5] Yet it was recognized that Jefferson in Paris and Adams in London would be engrossed with duties that would prevent either

---

[2] Writings, vol. iv, 376.
[3] Her crew was released by intervention of the court of Spain, but the vessel was abandoned (Carmichael to Jefferson, July 11, 1785, J. MSS.).
[4] Dip. Cor., vol. ii, p. 299.
[5] Richard Henry Lee to Jefferson, May 16, 1785, J. MSS.

from going to Africa. So a special agent was dispatched for the Moroccan negotiation. This agent was John Lamb, recommended to Congress by citizens of Connecticut; he had engaged in trade with Algiers and knew the country, although he spoke only English. No commission was furnished by Congress, but letters were written to Adams and Jefferson, and a set of instructions and the scheme of a treaty were sent by Lamb, who was expected to proceed on to Morocco under their directions.[6]

He was long on the way. The delay worried Jefferson so much that by the middle of August he decided to sound Adams on selecting a new envoy and giving both powers and instructions to him upon their own responsibility. Acting on his conviction, Jefferson drew up a project of a treaty, based in part on Franklin's scheme, sent it to Adams, and, overlooking the latter's rather timid objections, induced Thomas Barclay to go to Morocco to get it negotiated.[7] Half of the money designated for all the treaties should be saved for Algiers,— " they certainly possess more than one-half the whole power of the Pyratical states,"—and a half of the remainder, or twenty thousand, for Morocco, or a little more if they demanded it, on account of their nearness to the Atlantic trade. A flattering letter was prepared for the Emperor, largely of information on the political and diplomatic arrangements of the United States, with the assurance that any document signed by Barclay would be agreeable to the ministers and would probably be ratified by Congress.[8]

Lamb arrived in London before Barclay could get ready to leave. The plan he brought from Congress was so similar to the one already prepared by Jefferson that only a few verbal changes were needed to render them identical. Although Jefferson and Adams were suspicious of Lamb, they agreed to give him a commission and instructions similar to those

[6] Jefferson to Adams, Sept. 24, 1785, J. MSS.; G. W. Allen, Our Navy and the Barbary Corsairs, p. 30.
[7] Eighth Report of Commissioners, Dip. Cor., vol. ii, p. 331; Adams to Jefferson, Aug. 18, and Jefferson to Adams, Sept. 4, 1785, J. MSS.
[8] Dip. Cor., vol. ii, p. 332.

made out for Barclay, and send him to Algiers. As a check on his operations they attached P. R. Randall to the mission and required that all expense money should be drawn for on Adams with indications of its use on each order. The outstanding features of the proposed treaties, many merely hopeful gestures, were the most favored nation principle, protection of commerce by passports and cargo certificates, release of captives, freedom in trade, and consular jurisdiction for American consuls.[9] The urgency of entering on these measures was forcibly proven during the very time they were suspended, for in the last week of June the Algerian xebecs found their first American victims. The schooner *Maria,* Captain Isaac Stevens, from Boston to Cadiz, was taken on June 25, and the ship *Dauphin,* Captain Richard O'Brien, on June 30, fifty leagues west of Lisbon, the combined crews numbering twenty-one.[10]

With Barclay was associated Colonel William Franks. They proceeded to Spain to advise with Carmichael, who was influential enough with the Spanish court to interest the king and the chief minister, Count de Florida Blanca, in the affair. Here they spent a leisurely two and a half months, soliciting favors from these officials. With letters from the king to the Emperor of Morocco, and from Florida Blanca to several Spanish officials in Africa, they left Cadiz on May 27, arriving at Mogadore five days later. Although they were well received, Barclay changed his earlier idea of certain success when he found many ceremonies and a greed for presents opposing him;[11] but the negotiations were speedily finished when he reached Morocco. The emperor suggested that as he had a satisfactory treaty with Spain he would have it copied with "United States" in place of "Spain," but Barclay's negative on this proposal was more firm than polite. He reminded the

---

[9] Ibid. This was October 5 to 11, 1785.
[10] Allen, p. 29; Carmichael to Jefferson, Sept. 2, 1785, and Feb. 3, 1786, J. MSS. He reported five ships taken.
[11] He had some time before asserted his willingness to go on from Morocco to Algiers, and if need be, to Constantinople (Dip. Cor., vol. iii, p. 79).

emperor that he had traveled far to execute this commission and if tribute, as in the Spanish treaty, was to replace friendship, he would stop at once.[12]   He not only won his point but succeeded in having the plan furnished by Jefferson and Adams adopted without material change.   He then made his way back along the coast from Mogadore to Tangier, appointing three brothers,—Francisco, Joseph, and Guelamo Chiappi,—as American agents at Morocco, Mogadore, and Tangier, respectively.[13]

The Moroccan treaty of 1787 was the first between a Christian state and a Barbary power that did not specify an annual tribute.[14]   Its twenty-five articles were naturally devoted to the protection of the nationals and the vessels of the United States in or near Morocco, and in each section it exhibited the fear of dangers it would guard against, not alone in the one but in all of the pirate countries.   The tenth article was amended to prevent the Moroccans from joining the other Moors with whom the United States might wage war,—a rather unnecessary safeguard in view of the coolness between the emperor and the Algerian dey.   If, on the other hand, trade should continue unhampered, the treaty was capable of promoting it by a most-favored-nation provision, as well as by many of the rules incorporated in our French and Dutch treaties.[15]   An added article contained the emperor's voluntary promise to protect the ships, goods, and persons of

---

[12] Barclay to Adams and Jefferson, Sept. 10 and 13, 1786, J. MSS. These letters, about thirty pages of manuscript, give details of Moroccan government, commerce, religion, captures, and other points of information, as well as an account of the negotiations.   Barclay was fortunate in selecting as interpreter a certain Fennish who proved to be adviser as well as translator.

[13] In a letter from Mogadore to Adams, July 30, 1786, enclosed in the J. MSS., Barclay said that he had used only $3,500 of the $20,000 allowed.   This did not, however, include his salary nor that of Franks, and some incidentals.   July 13, 1787, Barclay sent to Adams and Jefferson two account books with all details of expenses. The total was 95,179 livres, 10 sols, which at the then rate of exchange of 24 livres to the pound, amounted to about 3,966 pounds.

[14] E. Dupuy, Americains et Barbaresques, p. 34.

[15] A version of this treaty is in Sec. Jour., vol. iii, pp. 348-362.   It was ratified by Congress, July 18, 1787.   On article XIV, see Menier, Traité de Commerce Franco-Americain, p. 26.

Americans,—a contribution that Barclay attributed to a sincere good disposition towards the United States.[16]

Lamb and Randall preceded Barclay to Spain. Their instructions were the same as had been given Barclay except for supplementary advices on the matter of captives. Jefferson added these on his own responsibility, but made it clear that if the two masters of the captured vessels wished to obligate themselves to repay Congress for their ransom, Lamb should be governed by their desires. There was apparently no anticipation of success in this mission, however much it might be wished. The Algerians were looked upon as more cruel, more avaricious, and more dangerous than any of the pirates.[17] So there was more need of Spanish influence than there had been in the case of Morocco; but in this application Carmichael and Lamb found Florida Blanca and D'Espilly indifferent if not actually hostile. " The day after their own affairs should be arranged with Algiers, his Catholic Majesty would employ his influence to facilitate our accommodation," Florida Blanca told Carmichael.[18]   And that his influence was not potent enough to be reassuring was seen in the fact that Spain's peace was understood to be costing her a million and a half dollars. Lamb and Randall waited in Spain " without reluctance " while Carmichael importuned the ministers for an introduction to the dey, and, in spite of the advice that they should wait until the outcome of the Spanish-Algerian negotiations was seen, sent them on to Barcelona with no entree prepared.[19]   Lamb bought a vessel at this port, and, under Spanish colors, he and Randall sailed for Algiers, arriving on March 25.

---

[16] Barclay to Adams, July 30, 1786, J. MSS.
[17] Note Jefferson's fear of having his second daughter come to France by any other than an English or French vessel (Jefferson to Francis Eppes, Dec. 11, 1785, J. MSS.).   The fear was exhibited in America by the rumor that Franklin had been captured on his way home (Allen, op. cit., p. 28; Otto to Jefferson, Jan. 15, 1786, J. MSS.; Monroe to Jefferson, Jan. 19, 1786, Monroe, Writings, vol. i, p. 112).
[18] Carmichael to Jefferson and Adams, Feb. 3, 1786, J. MSS.
[19] Dip. Cor., vol. iii, p. 33.   But see Carmichael's letter to Jefferson, June 16, 1786, for excuses, J. MSS.

This mission was a total failure. Lamb was controlled by his preconceived fears and Randall was disgusted with the adventure. The day after they were allowed to land was set for an audience, but it was prevented by a rain storm. A consultation with the Spanish, French, and English consuls resulted in divided counsel; and when the dey notified them that if their business concerned peace, and if they had no treaty with Constantinople, he would not give them any official recognition, Lamb practically gave up.[20] He decided to send Randall back to Paris to report the refusal. " I asked Mr. Lamb what I could say to the Minister except that the Dey had refused to treat of peace and most earnestly requested it as a favor—but he would make me no reply or give me any instructions." [21]   The purpose of insisting on a treaty with the Porte was to prevent Spain from interceding for Portugal and Naples since they had no such treaties. But this political dodge was much less important than the amount of money the dey and his council demanded. Vergennes, disagreeing with D'Espilly, scoffed at the Turkish treaty: " The Barbary States," he said, " acknowledged a sort of vassalage to the Porte, and availed themselves of that relation when anything was to be gained by it; but, that whenever it subjected them to a demand from the Porte, they totally disregarded it; that money was the sole agent at Algiers, except so far as fear could be induced also." [22]

Lamb had interviews with the dey on April 3, 7, and 17. The main item of discussion was the price for the release of the twenty-one American captives, which Lamb found " far beyond my limits" although the dey " fell something of his first price." [23]   The chief minister explained that these sums

---

[20] Randall's letter, April 2, 1786, J. MSS. This is a copy by Short. It omits the address. Lamb to Jefferson, May 20, 1786, Dip. Cor., vol. iii, p. 81. But see J. MSS., same date, for correct copy; O'Brien to Jefferson, Sept. 25, 1787, J. MSS.

[21] Randall's letter, April 2, 1786, J. MSS.

[22] Quoted in Jefferson's letter to Jay, May 23, 1786, Dip. Cor., vol. iii, p. 48. Vergennes had been ambassador from France to Turkey from 1754 to 1768.

[23] Lamb to Jefferson, May 20, 1786, J. MSS. The price for captains was $6,000 each; for mates, $4,000; passengers, $4,000; sailors,

were demanded in order to make the tribute levied on Spain appear moderate, and advised Lamb to return to Spain and await a more favorable opportunity. This advice appeared the more reasonable to Lamb when he saw that D'Espilly was suppressing a letter from the King of Spain,—a belated contribution by Carmichael for Lamb's introduction,—and when it appeared that no help could be expected from the French or English consuls.[24] Leaving his vessel to D'Espilly's care, as well as four hundred dollars for the relief of the captives, Lamb fled from the plague-infested country and came back to Alicante, relishing even the long quarantine there more than further conversations with Algerian officials.

The inconsequential outcome of this mission convinced Jefferson of the futility of using diplomacy with Algiers. He dismissed the hope of making a treaty of amity and commerce with a state that had neither friends nor commerce, and fell back on the problem of getting the Americans out of captivity, and the equally difficult problem of how to bring a greater force than money on a people whose only impulses came from money and fear. He learned from Randall that they had but nine war ships; that their reputation for skillful handling of these was considerably exaggerated; and that, while strong at close quarters, in his opinion six ships of the line and five or six hundred well disciplined men would be able to destroy their power.[25] A greater naval authority, Count D'Estaing, informed him that, a few years before, a Captain Massiac proposed to reduce Algiers by a continuous cruise and blockade, shutting up the harbor with a spliced cable. D'Estaing believed the idea was feasible, more so than bombardments.[26] A combination of powers blockading the pirates constantly for a few years would, he believed, force them " to become merchants in spite of themselves."

$1,400. Including the customary eleven per cent added to ransoms, this totalled $59,496, about $20,000 more than Lamb had to offer. An imperfect copy of this letter is in Dip. Cor., vol. iii, p. 81.

[24] Dupuy, p. 42.

[25] Randall's letter.

[26] D'Estaing said: " Bombardments are but transitory. It is, if I may so express myself, like breaking glass windows with guineas." Massiac succeeded in considerable measure (Dip. Cor., vol. iii, p. 110).

Realizing that nothing more could be accomplished at the time, Jefferson and Adams decided to call Lamb and Randall back to Paris and London, learn what details had not been given in letters, and send them on to New York to put the whole matter before Congress, whose wisdom would have to decide whether further negotiations should be undertaken.[27] But Lamb dodged the issue. In fact he hid away, even from Carmichael, ran off to the island of Minorca when Barclay went to Alicante to audit his accounts and offered the excuse of ill health for not going either to Paris or New York. Adams shut off his credit and both ministers gave him orders to report either to them or to Congress.[28] In a joint letter to him they wrote:

> The importance of peace with the Algerines and the other inhabitants of the coast of Barbary, to the United States renders it necessary that every information which can be obtained should be laid before Congress. And as the demands for the redemption of captives as well as the amount of customary presents are so much more considerable than seem to have been expected in America it appears to us necessary that you should return without loss of time to New York, there to give an account to Congress of all the particulars which have come to your knowledge as well as of your own proceedings and of the monies which have been paid on account of the United States in consequence of your draughts upon their Minister in London.[29]

At the end of 1786 Jefferson forwarded Congress' official recall of Lamb, in a letter to Carmichael, asking him to deliver it. Yet it was not until late in the next May that Lamb finally left Spain for America, leaving as his last message to Jefferson, a warning against D'Espilly who, he said, had blocked all his efforts at Algiers.[30]

---

[27] Jefferson to Adams, Dip. Cor., vol. iii, p. 20; Jefferson to Adams, May 30, 1786, J. MSS.; Randall to Adams and Jefferson, May 14, 1786, ibid.; Adams to Jefferson, May 23, Works, vol. viii, p. 393; Lamb to Jefferson, June 6, 1786, J. MSS.

[28] Jefferson to Lamb, June 20, 1786, J. MSS.; Adams to Lamb, June 29, Works, vol. viii, p. 405. Carmichael wrote Jefferson that Mrs. Lamb, then in America, had obtained money on Lamb's letter of credit (Jefferson to Adams, Oct. 23, 1786, J. MSS.).

[29] Adams and Jefferson to Lamb, June 29, in London, July 7, in Paris, 1786, J. MSS.

[30] Sec. Jour., vol. iv, p. 127; Dip. Cor., vol. iii, pp. 186, 257; Montgomery to Jefferson, May 22 and 26, 1787, J. MSS. Jefferson

During the summer and fall of 1786 it was considered possible that either Barclay or Carmichael might take up the negotiations that Lamb had abandoned. But Adams did not favor the suggestion, however acceptable either of these men might have been, and his opinion had its influence with Jefferson.[31] There was no official sanction for them to commission any one. Moreover, Adams was controlled by the serious fact that there was no money to put any plan into execution; whereas Jefferson was guided by what he believed would eventually be necessary for a settled, satisfactory peace, and that was the use of force. Adams contended that the loss to our commerce was equal to the price that would buy peace, and further that even after an immensely expensive armament should have been sent to the Mediterranean, we should still have to pay as much, probably more, money to the pirates. Jefferson agreed that it would cost a considerable amount in any case, but honor and self-respect, in addition to a smaller expense and greater effectiveness, required war. Besides, the United States ought to have a navy. And, finally, his strongest point was the undeniable fact that a paid-for peace had always proved unreliable, broken without notice, and each year more expensive to maintain.[32]

Without money enough to buy a peace, or a navy to command one, there was but one resource for the United States, so Jefferson believed, and that was to combine with European powers to eliminate the Barbary menace entirely. Most agreeable to this idea among the nations was Portugal, whose queen nad already ordered her fleet to protect American as well as Portuguese vessels from the pirates, and with whom a commercial treaty was then under way.[33] But Portugal was lack-

---

took the blame for sending Lamb to Algiers, but Adams believed they were both blameless (Jefferson to Adams, Dec. 20, 1786, and Adams to Jefferson, Jan. 25, 1787, J. MSS.). Carmichael retained his confidence in D'Espilly (Dip. Cor., vol. iii, p. 121).

[31] Jefferson to Adams, Sept. 26, 1786, J. MSS.

[32] Adams to Jefferson, July 3, 1786, Works, vol. viii, p. 406; Jefferson to Adams, July 11, 1786, Dip. Cor., vol. iii, p. 108; Allen, p. 35; Jay to Jefferson, Dec. 14, 1786, ibid., p. 133.

[33] Adams to Jefferson, June 29, 1786, and entries under dates of Nov. 27, 1785, and Aug. 11, 1786, J. MSS.

ing in power, and the same was true of Naples, reported by
Carmichael as willing to join.[34]   Moreover such states were
dependent on the pressure and policies of the major powers
when action in the Mediterranean was concerned.   Jefferson
was at last reacting to the suspicions poured in on him that
the agents of Spain, England, France, and Holland were
secretly thwarting all American efforts in Algiers.[35]   To
throw the whole matter into open view of the world, to secure
united international police action on it, and to save for his
own nation humiliation and expense, Jefferson worked out a
scheme for concerted action against the Barbary states, with
Algiers as the first victim.   Its object was to compel and
guarantee peace, without price, by means of a naval force in
perpetual cruise, with quotas arranged reasonably among
members of the league, probably not exceeding half a dozen
frigates.   This " league of nations " was to be managed by a
council of ambassadors meeting at such a convenient center
as Versailles, and the agreement was to hold regardless of
other warfare, but was not to affect existing treaties with the
Barbary states.[36]   This proposition was introduced into
Congress during July of the following year and the motion
ordering American participation was carried with only three
dissenting votes,[37]—an interesting action considering the opposition to " entangling alliances " of succeeding years.

Small enthusiasm arose in Europe over Jefferson's proposal, and he was the more convinced that peace with Algiers
was not an immediate prospect.   Besides, making a treaty
was a different matter from securing the release of the Americans held captive.   The latter was an object of pressing
necessity, to which Jefferson turned, taking, as usual, the lead
over Adams.   He found that an order of begging priests,—
the Mathurins,—undertook commissions of redeeming prisoners in Algiers.   He sounded their " general " with regard to

[34] Dip. Cor., vol. iii, p. 129.
[35] Dip. Cor., vol. ii, pp. 243, 286, vol. iii, pp. 14, 33, 55; Langdon
to Jefferson, Dec. 7, 1785; Jefferson to Gen. Greene, Jan. 12, 1786;
Randall's letter; O'Brien to Carmichael, Sept. 13, 1786, J. MSS.
[36] J. MSS., Nov., 1786.   [37] Sec. Jour., vol. iv, p. 472.

the American captives. This was broached to Adams and was by him opposed on the ground that no government redeemed prisoners except at the time of making peace, and he and Jefferson as "subordinate ministers" had no right to establish a precedent. Besides, the Barbary expenses had to be brought to a full stop. Lamb had drawn 3,212 pounds, and Barclay 7,020, and money was needed for interest on our European debts.[38]

After Lamb's retirement from Algiers, the support for the Americans in captivity was furnished by the Count D'Espilly, whose advances made it incumbent on Jefferson to take some measures to meet the situation when Lamb's powers were brought to an end. The distance of Paris from Algiers, as well as from America, the lack of information, and most of all, the lack of money, made it difficult for Jefferson to decide on an expeditious policy. He referred it to Jay for the decision of Congress, mentioning the Mathurins, and advising that the first redemption be at a low price to avoid arousing the cupidity of the pirates. He even assumed that it would be wise to appear to neglect the captives altogether, and to conduct all operations for their release secretly and without their knowledge.[39] When it came up for action, Congress admitted its inability to decide and referred the redemption to Jefferson with advice to follow such measures as he deemed advisable, ordering the treasury board to furnish ways and means to meet the expense.[40] Thus Jefferson was obliged to assume responsibility for solving the Barbary problem as well as devising plans to subsist the captives until they could be released.

The situation was rendered practically hopeless by two developments. In the first place the plague raged in Algiers with terrible effects during the summers of 1787 and 1788. Montgomery was authority for a statement that from January first to August twenty-fifth, 1787, it carried off 18,000

---

[38] Dip. Cor., vol. iii, p. 207.
[39] Ibid., vol. iii, p. 208; Jefferson to Adams, Feb. 6, 1787, J. MSS.
[40] See. Jour., vol. iv, p. 348.

Mohammedans, 1,800 Jews, and 640 Christian slaves.[41] This, of course, caused a cessation of summer cruising and so reduced the number of captives as to raise the price on those left alive. The other feature was acquiescence by Spain and other Mediterranean states in the higher redemption prices. At the time Lamb went to Algiers, the average sum was $200 for each captive; at the end of 1788 it was about $1200. This was beyond the ability, or at least the disposition, of the United States to pay, even though the number of Americans in captivity had been reduced from twenty-one to fifteen.[42]

The plan of pretending neglect was also broken down by several volunteer efforts to arrange for redemption. It was rumored that Lamb had promised to return with the ransom demanded, that is, $59,496. Later the firm of Bulkleys, of Lisbon, contracted for those still alive, at $34,792; and M. Cathalan, American consul at Marseilles, essayed to conduct a private negotiation. The total results of these attempts were to place on American captives " the highest prices ever paid by any nation; and thus these charitable, though unauthorized interpositions, have had the double effect of lengthening the chains they were meant to break, and of making us at last set a much higher rate of ransom for our citizens, present and future, than we probably should have obtained if we had been left alone to do our own work, in our own way." [43]

The actual care of the captives Jefferson took from Carmichael and turned over to the Mathurins.

As the General of the Mathurins was to be employed in the final redemption of our captives, I thought that their previous support had better be put into his hands, and conducted by himself in such a way as not to counterwork his plan of redemption, whenever we can enable him to begin on it. I gave him full powers as to the amount and manner of subsisting them. He has undertaken it, informing me at the same time, that it will be on a very low scale, to avoid suspicion of its coming from the public.[44]

As soon as money was provided, Jefferson entrusted the head of the Mathurins with the business and put under his com-

[41] Montgomery to Jefferson, Aug. 25, 1787, J. MSS.
[42] Dip. Cor., vol. iii, p. 439.
[43] Am. St. P., For. Rel., vol. i, p. 291.
[44] Jefferson to Jay, Jan. 11, 1789, Dip. Cor., vol. iv, p. 47.

mand the amount of 3,000 livres for each captive, with instructions to proceed as seemed best; if necessary, to send a member of the order to Marseilles at the expense of the United States.[45]

This was shortly before Jefferson's departure for America. His experience of four years' dealing with the pirate nations is epitomized in a letter to John Paul Jones, in which his original conclusions of force and combined action are not changed:

You know my sentiments respecting the Algerines. I shall certainly make them a subject of consultation with our government while I shall be in America. My favorite project is still to procure a concurrence of the powers at war with them, that that concurrence continue till the strength of those barbarians at sea be totally annihilated, and that the combined force employed in effecting this shall not be disturbed in its operation by wars or other incidents occurring between the powers composing it.[46]

And Captain O'Brien, who had furnished Jefferson with so much information on Algiers, and who had regularly advocated a paid-for peace, in preference to a forced peace, was changing his views, for he wrote, " in my opinion, until the Algerines more strictly adhere to the Treaties they have already made, it would be impolitic in any nation to try to make a peace here; for I see that they take more from the nations they are at peace with than they do from those that they are at declared war with." [47]

When Jefferson came into the office of Secretary of State, another motive was added to those he had felt while he was in France, and it called for more energy in clearing up this troublesome business. This was the pressure of commercial firms for provision to safeguard American ships in the Mediterranean. It was asserted that from fifty to one hundred vessels would immediately enter that trade as soon as they had any assurance of protection.[48] The initial action would

---

[45] Jefferson to M. Chauvier, General de l'Ordre de Sainte Trinité, Sept., 1789, J. MSS.
[46] March 23, 1789, J. MSS.
[47] O'Brien to Jefferson, June 13, 1789, J. MSS. But the Emperor of Morocco released a vessel taken at this time (Dip. Cor., vol. iv, p. 130).
[48] Letter from a " Merchant in Maryland," March 28, 1790; Edward Rutledge to Jefferson, April 28, 1790, J. MSS.

have to come from America, for the Mathurins had gone into eclipse in the French Revolution, and none of the American agents in Europe were to be considered as capable of handling the problem.[49]   Yet Jefferson realized that there was no action he could take that would not call for an appropriation, and it was to put the matter before Congress that he kept agitating it during the summer and fall of 1790.   At the same time O'Brien was redoubling his efforts in Algiers and, according to his own reports, seemed to be fairly successful in getting a hearing and even a tentative agreement on ransom.[50]   So that when Washington included a reference to the relief of trade in the Mediterranean, in his address to Congress on December 8, 1790, evidence was given that the much-delayed solution was about to be found.   A week later the House of Representatives called on Jefferson for a report on this branch of American commerce.

The reply was prompt and exhaustive.   He showed by statistics the importance of that trade, gave a summary of what had been done to relieve the situation while he was in Europe, and set forth his views on the three possible courses to pursue to bring a satisfactory conclusion to the whole Barbary matter.[51]   Dismissing Tunis and Tripoli as comparatively unimportant, he pointed out that dependence for protection against Algiers might be placed in insurance on ships and cargoes and a convention for redeeming captives at a fixed rate.   This plan would still leave the terrors of slavery, of the plague, and of delays to shipping, so that our commerce would seek less dangerous paths and hence abandon the Mediterranean altogether.   The second plan was to purchase peace.   The various estimates by persons who had been in Algiers and were conversant with conditions there, placed the amount at not less than three hundred thousand, nor more than a million, dollars, inclusive of all items.   But

[49] Short to Jefferson, June 4 and 25, 1790, J. MSS.
[50] O'Brien to Carmichael, June 24, and O'Brien to Jefferson, July 12, 1790, J. MSS.
[51] Dec. 28, 1790.   In this report he stated that the cost of the Moroccan treaty was only $10,000.   But see page 24, above.

Jefferson pointed out that the experience of European nations made an annual tribute a more effective and economical method, although neither plan carried a guarantee of good faith nor assurance of accomplishing its purpose.

The third expedient was war. To match the whole naval force of Algiers and to meet them at their own game, namely cruising, was within the power of the United States. Jefferson did not venture to recommend a detailed plan for this action since that recommendation belonged to the war department rather than to his own, but he did suggest the idea of continual cruising and called attention to the success of the Portuguese who, by this method, had succeeded in keeping the Algerian xebecs out of the Atlantic.

Jefferson felt that the occasion also demanded an answer to the appeal of the captives. Consequently he prepared a report for the president which chronicled the events of the captures and the attempts at ransom. The various prices demanded and offered for ransom ran from two hundred to two thousand nine hundred and twenty dollars for each man, only one of whom,—a Scotch boy,—had been released at that date. For the liberation of the remaining fourteen it would require from eighteen to thirty-five thousand dollars, unless by assuming an aggressive character Americans could capture Moors and exchange prisoners. At any rate, Jefferson forced Congress and the president to assume responsibility; all his information was placed before both, and possible plans pointed out to relieve a distressing state of affairs. That ransom and relief of trade were coupled was Jefferson's belief; the remedy for one would cure both ills. " The liberation of our citizens has an intimate connection with the liberation of our commerce in the Mediterranean, now under consideration of Congress. The distresses of both proceed from the same cause, and the measures which shall be adopted for the relief of the one, may very probably involve the relief of the other." [52]

The death of the Emperor of Morocco occasioned the neces-

[52] " Report of the Secretary of State to the President on the matter of American captives held by the Algerines," Dec. 28, 1790, J. MSS.

sity of getting the treaty with that country acknowledged by his successor, and on this Congress was ready to act more quickly than on the peace with Algiers. Early in March, 1791, twenty thousand dollars was appropriated and Thomas Barclay was commissioned to proceed to Morocco, in the character of consul, to seek recognition of the treaty and to gain the good disposition of the new emperor. Colonel David Humphreys, United States resident at Lisbon, was given control of the funds, of which half was allotted, by secret instructions, for " presents." [53]   On Barclay's arrival in Europe, he found that the claimants to the Moroccan throne had involved that country in civil war, and since none of them gave appearance of final success, he could do nothing but remain in Spain and await the outcome.

Delay in this quarter was matched by delay on the Algerian peace. For the remainder of 1791 nothing was done except to transfer the control of the captives at Algiers to Carmichael and Humphreys, and to instruct the former to verify and pay the account of D'Espilly for their past subsistence.[54]   In November a report on ransom was submitted to the House of Representatives, as the result of the petition of a Charles Colvill to recover money for ransom and traveling expenses; and on December 2 the draft of a secret resolution for Senate action was sent in to that body. This was referred to a committee and gained the response Jefferson was seeking. Senator Butler and his committee conferred with the president; they asked Jefferson to draw up a bill authorizing the president to appoint a special envoy to Algiers, but confessed that the Senate could not get funds without the " agency " of the Representatives, and so were " afraid to make the Com[n]." Jefferson explained, in a written opinion to the president, that he believed the lower house should be consulted, regardless of secrecy, for while a treaty was the law of the land yet

[53] Am. St. P., For. Rel., vol. i, p. 289.
[54] D'Espilly's account had been bought by one Don Joseph Iorino, of Madrid (Jefferson to Humphreys, July 13; Iorino to Jefferson, Dec. 12; Jefferson to de Viar, Dec. 13; Jefferson to Humphreys, Dec. 13, all 1791, J. MSS.).

it required execution, and action necessary for execution depended on the will of the representatives.[55]

The result was a resolution in the Senate on May 8, 1792, adopting the plan of annual tribute. The resolution ran:

" Resolved, That if the President of the United States shall conclude a treaty with the government of Algiers for the establishment of peace with them at an expense not exceeding forty thousand dollars paid at the signature, and a sum not exceeding twenty-five thousand dollars to be paid annually afterwards, during the continuance of the treaty, the Senate will approve the same. And in case such treaty be concluded, and the President of the United States shall also conclude a convention, or treaty, with the Government of Algiers, for the ransom of the thirteen Americans in captivity there, for a sum not exceeding forty thousand dollars, all expenses included, the Senate will also approve such convention or treaty." [56]

Accordingly three commissions were made out to John Paul Jones to act as envoy in concluding a treaty of peace, in making a convention for ransom, and to be American consul at Algiers. In the long, detailed set of instructions, Jefferson made Jones acquainted with all preceding steps and the reasoning by which the plan of annual tribute was adopted. The amount appropriated by Congress was fifty thousand dollars, so that Jefferson felt obliged to allot different sums to peace and to ransom from those indicated by the Senate's arrangement. For the first yearly payment, twenty-five thousand dollars was allowed; for ransom, twenty-seven thousand; and for salary and expenses of the envoy, three thousand. Money, and not naval stores, was to be used. A copy of the Moroccan treaty was enclosed as a model for this negotiation, with recommendation to insert an article on Tunis and Tripoli, if Algiers were willing to use influence to protect Americans there. The sum for ransom was based on O'Brien's

---

[55] Washington to Jefferson, March 10; Notes, March 11 and April 10, 1792, J. MSS.

[56] Am. St. P., For. Rel., vol. i, p. 290.

advices; and his cooperation in the coming negotiations was urged on Admiral Jones. Jefferson could not resist inserting a clause characteristic of his own conclusions:

" As the duration of this peace cannot be counted on with certainty, and we look forward to the necessity of coercion, by cruizes on their coast, to be kept up during the whole of their cruizing season, you will be pleased to inform yourself as minutely as possible, of every circumstance which may influence or guide us in undertaking and conducting such an operation, making your communications by safe opportunities." [57]

These papers and the funds to expedite the mission were confided to the care of Thomas Pinckney, then going as United States Minister to London, and in case Admiral Jones would not perform the duty assigned to him, his place was to be filled by Barclay. When Pinckney arrived in London, he learned of the death of Admiral Jones. He endeavored to find means of transferring the papers to Barclay, but was delayed by a lack of safe conveyance, and shortly after they were delivered, Barclay was stricken by " fever of the lungs," and died on January 19, 1793. His death was not known in America until March, when the president appointed Colonel Humphreys to take up the negotiations, first settling Barclay's public business. With him, as secretary, was associated Captain Nathaniel Cutting. Care of the money was still left to Pinckney. Humphreys anticipated part of this commission, having hurried to Gibraltar to look after the public property under Barclay's control, and he was waiting at that place for a favorable opportunity to go on to Algiers when a disastrous turn took place in American-Barbary relations.[58] Portugal, for years the main reliance of American shippers against the menace of Algiers, suddenly concluded a peace with the pirates, and, as Jefferson reported: " Whatever expectations might have been formed of the issue of the mission to Algiers,

---

[57] Ibid., vol. i, p. 292.
[58] For a later mission, or proposed mission, see F. L. Nussbaum, Commercial Policy in the French Revolution, p. 309.

at its first projection, or the subsequent renewals to which unfortunate events gave accession, they must now be greatly diminished, if not entirely abandoned. While the truce with two such commercial nations as Portugal and Holland has so much lessened the number of vessels exposed to the capture of these corsairs, it has opened the door which lets them out upon our commerce, and ours alone; as, with the other nations navigating the Atlantic, they are at peace. Their first successes will probably give them high expectations of future advantage, and leave them little disposed to relinquish them on any terms." [59]

This unfortunate consummation, just as Jefferson was leaving the state department, was a deep disappointment to him. The illogical move of Congress in trying to secure peace and ransoms at once, though possibly more economical, the delay from 1790 to 1792 in preparing means for a mission, and the knowledge of the bitter feeling among the captives at their neglect, caused him to vindicate his course in a letter of March 22, 1793, to Colonel David:

I do not wonder that Capt. O'Brien has lost patience under his long-continued captivity, & that he may suppose some of the public servants have neglected him & his brethren. He may possibly impute neglect to me, because a forbearance to correspond with him would have that appearance, tho' it was dictated by the single apprehension that if he received letters from me as M. P. of the U. S. at Paris, or as Secretary of State, it would increase the expectations of the captors and raise the ransom beyond what his countrymen would be disposed to give, & so end in their perpetual captivity. But in truth I have labored for them constantly, & zealously in every situation in which I have been placed. In the first moment of their captivity, I first proposed to Mr. Adams to take upon ourselves their ransom, tho' unauthorized by Congress, I proposed to Congress & obtained their permission to employ the order of Mercy in France for their ransom, but never could obtain orders for the money till just as I was leaving France & was obliged to turn the matter over to Mr. Short. As soon as I came here I laid the matter before the President & Congress in two long reports, but Congress could not decide till the beginning of 1792, & then clogged their ransom by a previous requisition of peace. The unfortunate deaths of two successive commissioners have still retarded their relief, &, even should they be now relieved, will probably deprive me of the gratification of seeing my endeavors for them crowned at length with success by their arrival while I am here.[60]

[59] Am. St. P., For. Rel., vol. i, p. 295.
[60] J. MSS.

4

CHAPTER III.

FRENCH-AMERICAN COMMERCE

The greater part of the manifold duties falling upon Jefferson while he was minister to France was consular rather than diplomatic. It was, in fact, due to exigencies of his nation and not to his own predilections that his efforts were shifted from the political to the economic, for Jefferson was a lawyer and not a business man. Yet it fell to his lot to become the first diplomatic agent of all time to apply the principles so recently set forth by Adam Smith in the "Wealth of Nations." That he had a Herculean task in attempting to break through the wall of European commercial exclusiveness is seen by even a casual glance at the French-American treaty of commerce of 1778. France, the friendliest of nations toward the United States, her only ally, at the moment of greatest generosity yielded nothing in an economic sense. The treaty provided for "the most perfect equality and reciprocity," but it did not mean abandonment by France of the maze of monopolies, prohibitions, fees, and particular privileges already characteristic of her commerce.

In approaching the French ministers and seeking new regulations for the trade between the two countries, Jefferson was placed in a peculiar position. The United States had not even established a thorough-going control over domestic commerce, although the proposition to amend the ninth section of the Articles of Confederation, as reported to Jefferson by Monroe, had a decided bearing on his attitude respecting the foreign trade of the United States. This was true not only in regard to his conception of the theoretical system, already mentioned,[1] but also in the practical steps he should take to assure a market for American products in France. Although sharing Monroe's bias in favor of the "southern" as against the "eastern" states, and always a particularist,

---

[1] Above, page 9.

yet he was entirely convinced that the control of foreign trade should be given to Congress. "My primary object in the formation of treaties is to take the commerce of the States out of the hands of the States and to place it under the superintendence of Congress, so far as the imperfect provisions of our Constitution will admit, and until the States shall, by new compact, make them more perfect." [2]

Disagreeing with the opinion of Adams that "we have already commercial advantages enough to satisfy a reasonable people," Jefferson began his attack on French monopolies by laying before Vergennes, in the summer of 1785, a summary of tobacco importations from the United States into France. He realized that he was touching a sensitive spot when he argued for relief from this monopoly, and hence directed his reasoning to the side of expansion of French national revenues. The retail price was too high, for a greater consumption with smaller tax would produce considerably more each year, and besides, payment in specie instead of by exports of goods was discouraging to industry. The seller, he said, carries his wares to the best market, not to that in which one buyer fixes the price. [3] The duty in English ports was higher, yet tobacco was carried there for liberty of sale. The danger of smuggling would be taken away as the selling price fell; and the other objection to the abolition of the Farm,—the lessened power to raise loans,—would have a slight foundation; possibly the loss would be one-eighth, but the gains would offset this.

This appeal had its effect on Vergennes. [4] But it was lessened by the bad feeling engendered in France by the acts of the States. The Massachusetts and New Hampshire legislatures, among others, excluded foreign vessels from all except four ports in each State. Marbois presented to Jay the memorial of protest these acts provoked among French mer-

[2] Writings, vol. iv, p. 421.
[3] Dip. Cor., vol. ii, p. 456.
[4] Nussbaum, "American Tobacco and French Politics, 1783-1793," in Political Science Quarterly, December, 1925.

chants.[5]   Vergennes wrote a blunt letter to Jefferson, asserting that this lack of reciprocity and the violation of the
treaty of 1778 would call for retaliation on France's part.
In answer, Jefferson was conciliatory. He pointed out that
a treaty on the most favored nation basis did not restrain
either party from discriminating between natives and foreigners; yet no more was done by the two States. A thing
exactly like it was accomplished by the *arrêts* of August 30,
1784, and September 18 and 25, 1785, and yet the French
ministers considered them as within the treaty.[6] But he
hoped the two States would repeal the laws. As he wrote
Adams: " the selfishness of England alone will not justify
our hazarding a contest of this kind against all Europe.
Spain, Portugal, and France have not yet shut their doors
against us; it will be time enough when they do to take up
the commercial hatchet." [7]

This disturbance was not serious enough, however, to stop
further negotiating on articles of trade. The application on
tobacco was allowed to mature and, at succeeding interviews
with Vergennes, Jefferson reviewed the whole range of mutual
exchange of goods. The matter of whale oil was pushed forward by Mr. Boylston, of Massachusetts, who protested to
Jefferson and Lafayette that he would be ruined if he were
obliged to pay the prevalent duties on his recent importation.
Jefferson convinced Lafayette of the advantage of securing
a general regulation on all such shipments rather than taking
one after the other as they came, and this was referred by
them to Calonne. The influence of the Marquis gained for

---

[5] Dip. Cor., vol. i, p. 234. The protest contained a peculiar point:
" Thirdly, although we may have the right and the disposition to
adopt rules analogous to the two laws of New Hampshire and
Massachusetts, we ought only to exercise this right with respect to
these two states, or the other eleven republics could say we have not
a right to exclude them from our ports by exorbitant impositions,
whilst they received us in theirs."

[6] Jefferson to Vergennes, Nov. 20, 1785, J. MSS.

[7] Nov. 19, 1785, J. MSS. In his confidential reports to Vergennes,
Otto mentioned the restrictions that the States, especially Virginia
and Massachusetts, had put on British commerce (French Transcripts, vol. xxxi, fol. 81, No. 36).

the proposal an order reducing the duty, for a year, from thirty-six to twelve livres, the same as paid by the merchants of the Hanse towns.[8] In replying to Lafayette, Calonne went on to ask some questions concerning American commercial policy. Was, he asked, freedom in trade to the French West Indies equally desirable or necessary to all of the States of the United States? Would the United States grant reciprocal commercial advantages for this liberty in colonial trade? Was it within the power of the United States to grant favors to one nation which they refused to another? If France should grant unlimited admittance to American goods at higher duties, these to be regained by obtaining French goods more freely, would the United States do the same for France, and would they consider themselves injured or favored? What advantages could Congress offer in return for what was solicited? If the United States received the liberties they asked, would they export only the least valuable objects to the West Indies, as a compensation, or would they allow France to have freedom of fishing on the northern coasts, and give preference to French woolens, linens, salt, and wine?[9]

It was against this attitude on the part of the Farmers-General that Jefferson had to struggle. Either this letter of Calonne's was a subterfuge, dodging the whole question, or else it was entirely impossible for the French minister to see the point in American policy. Jefferson did not want a commercial *alliance* with France, presenting a monopolistic demeanor toward the rest of the world. But so far as he could, without sacrificing everything to, and receiving nothing from, Great Britain, he wanted the most favored nation

---

[8] This was due, automatically, under the most favored nation clause of the treaty of 1778, and should have been applied for as a right, not as a privilege, a fact of which Jefferson was aware.

[9] Dip. Cor., vol. ii, p. 494. Jay wrote Jefferson, June 16, 1786: "When I was in France I heard that system censured by almost every gentleman whom I heard speak of it, and yet it seems so firmly fixed, perhaps by golden rivets, even on sovereignty itself, as that the speedy destruction of it seems rather to be wished for than expected" (Dip. Cor., vol. iii, p. 7).

principle working to free the principal commercial nations
from such practices, of separate, exclusive agreements whereby each nation was slave of opportunist and mercantilist
policies.

When Jefferson objected to the duties on American fish
brought to the French West Indies, Vergennes explained that
French fishermen could not furnish the entire supply; and
moreover the discrimination was not as great as appeared, for
differences in seasons favored the Americans, and other econo-
mies made a balance in favor of the latter equal to the duty
levied on them. But he hastened to change the subject, and,
with the aid of Reyneval, brought the discussion around to his
favorite charges against the United States,—their disregard
for treaties, their failure to meet obligations, and the injustice
to foreigners of their laws. The case in point, on the last of
these accusations, was the devolution of General Oglethorpe's
estate, to which a French subject, the Chevalier de Mézières,
was claimant, although the General's widow was then living.
Jefferson found "these ideas new, serious, and delicate."
Two legal points were involved. First, whether the Declaration of Independence had, in fact, made citizens of the
United States and British subjects alien to each other; and,
secondly, whether the legislature of Georgia had, by an act
of confiscation, unjustly taken away the chance of inheritance, and thus violated the treaty rights of the heirs.

Without actually committing himself to an express opinion,
Jefferson intimated his understanding that the Declaration
did have the effect indicated. On the second head, he demonstrated to Vergennes and Reyneval that de Mézières had
neither a conveyance of property nor a succession *ab intestato,*
that his rights were placed on the same basis as those of a
citizen of Georgia, which was certainly all that the treaty
could do. As to action by the Georgia legislature, he observed: "There was no occasion for the Assemblies to pass
laws on this subject, the treaty being a law, as I conceive,
superior to those of particular Assemblies, and repealing them
where they stand in the way of its operation." [10] His success

---

[10] Ibid.

in this was reported to Adams: "Monsieur de Reyneval having assured me that what I had written on that subject had perfectly satisfied the *Ct* de Vergennes and himself that this case could never come under the treaty." [11]

Reyneval gave the first suggestion of hope for abolition of the Farm by supporting Jefferson's proposition for its discontinuance.[12] Vergennes allowed it to go to the Comptroller, Calonne, where it met with a negative. It was impossible to remove the monopoly on tobacco, Calonne said, "without unravelling the whole transaction." Evidently this meant that the Comptroller held office by a precarious tenure. "The influence of the Farmers-General has heretofore been found sufficient to shake a minister in his office. Monsieur de Calonne's continuance or dismission has been thought for some time to be on a poise. The joint interests of France and America would be an insufficient counterpoise in his favor." [13]

These were not very effective blows at the roots of the monopoly. The outlook was darkened, at the beginning of 1786, when the Farmers made known a contract with Robert Morris giving him exclusive right to furnish all the tobacco brought from America, for three years and at a fixed price.[14] This would naturally fix the price for tobacco already in port, in France, in American vessels. Protests began to pour in on Jefferson who was thus spurred on to redouble his efforts. With further help from Lafayette, he succeeded in having the renewal of the Farm postponed for six months. Moreover, a committee was selected to examine Morris's contract and to estimate its effects. The conclusions of this committee,[15] made public orders on May 30, 1786, prohibited future bargains of the same nature at the expiration of this contract;

---

[11] Feb. 7, 1786, J. MSS.

[12] Reyneval was not, however, a person in whom much trust could be placed (Jefferson to Madison, Jan. 30, 1787, Writings, vol. v, p. 254).

[13] Dip. Cor., vol. ii, p. 482.

[14] Jefferson to the Governor of Virginia, Jan. 24, 1786, J. MSS.

[15] Nussbaum, "American Tobacco and French Politics, 1783-1793," in Polit. Science Quart., Dec. 1925. It derived its name from the name of Calonne's chateau, "Bernis," where its meetings were held.

required the Farmers to purchase each year from twelve to fifteen thousand hogsheads in addition to the amount furnished by Morris, on the same terms as his; and restricted the importation to French and American vessels.[16]   But the double monopoly had its effects.   Jefferson estimated that the loss to Virginia and Maryland growers was 400,000 pounds a year.[17]   Nevertheless he sent notices of the new order to the Governors of Virginia and Maryland, to the American agents in French ports, and to American importers.[18]

Once started, the Committee continued to make a thorough analysis of the trade between France and the United States. As Lafayette was the leading member of it, Jefferson furnished him with information on the articles not comprehended in preceding *arrêts,* and in July sent him an account of the imports and exports of the United States, made up from customs house papers and his own estimates.   His tabulation was as follows:

EXPORTS

Articles	To Europe (in louis)	To the West Indies (in louis)
Fish	107,000	50,000
Fish oil	181,668	9,562
Live stock	————	99,000
Salted meats	————	131,500
Flour and bread	330,000	330,000
Wheat	331,000	————
Rice	189,350	70,650
Tobacco	1,305,000	————
Peltry	184,900	
Lumber	82,000	164,000
Ships	216,500	————
All others [19]	375,030	86,840
	3,302,448	941,552

Total Exports...... 4,244,000

[16] Dip. Cor., vol. iii, pp. 59, 68; Jefferson to James Ross, May 8; Jefferson to Vergennes, May 3; Jefferson to Otto, May 7, 1786, all J. MSS.   Morris's importations were restricted to American vessels alone.

[17] Jefferson to Adams, July 9, 1786, J. MSS.

[18] Jefferson to the Governor of Virginia and to the Governor of Maryland, May 31; to William McCarty, May 15; to L. Coffyn, June 4; to Portas, Carnes, Bondfield, Cathalan, Alexander, Paradise, (agents and importers), June 6 to Aug. 8, 1786, all J. MSS.

[19] Many smaller items in Jefferson's list are here brought together.

IMPORTS

From Europe	From West Indies
Woolens, linens, hats, shoes, silks, lace, brass, tin, iron, wine, books, slaves, salt, etc. 3,039,000	Rum, sugar, Molasses, mahogany, salt, cocoa, cotton, etc. 927,438

Total Imports...... 3,966,438

After due allowance is made for diplomatic courtesies, it appears that Jefferson and Lafayette, working through this committee, produced a powerful influence on the trade of their respective nations. It was a turning point in French-American relations, loosening rather than cementing the alliance. In late October, Calonne wrote Jefferson a summary of the ministerial views on all subjects which had been reviewed, with as much emphasis as possible on the relaxation in regulations or duties. Exportation of brandies was freed; the *droit du Roi et d'Ameraute* was reduced, but any change in the tobacco duties was refused; on whale oil a further reduction was granted,—" His Majesty consents to abolish the duty of fabrication, with respect to the whale and spermaceti directly imported from the United States, in French or American bottoms, so that this oil and spermaceti shall not pay during ten years any other duty but 7 livres, 10 sols per livre, this last augmentation of ten sols per livre shall cease in 1790." [20]

Complete abolition of duties was ordered on potash, pearlash, beaver skins, leather, furs, and all kinds of wood useful for ship timbers. Moreover, the purchase of American-built ships was brought under the same rule. And, " whenever the United States shall think it expedient to export from France, arms, guns, and gunpowder, they shall have full permission, provided these articles are exported in French or American

[20] Dip. Cor., vol. iii, pp. 154, 162. At about the same time, in a letter to de Warville, when offering corrections for his work on the commerce between France and the United States, Jefferson said: " When you proceed to form your table of American exports and imports, I make no doubt you will consult the American traveller, the estimates in which are nearer the truth than those of Lord Sheffield and Deane, as far as my knowledge of the facts enables me to judge " (Aug. 16, 1786, J. MSS.).

vessels, and they shall be liable only to a very small duty, in order to facilitate the calculation of exports." [21]

Sketching out some " observations " on this letter, Jefferson could find but few objections to the rulings, aside, of course, from the subject of tobacco. He learned, for example, that while potash was exempted from national duties, yet the city of Rouen taxed it twenty sols per quintal. This shut out Americans from the trade which supplied the soap and glass factories near Paris. Materials that were shipped in raw or near-raw state, he believed, ought to be entirely exempted from duties since they could least bear charges.[22] Forwarding Calonne's letter to Jay, he observed : " We may consider them [the regulations] as an ultimate settlement of the conditions of our commerce with this country, for though the consolidation of ship duties and the encouragements for the importation of rice, are not finally decided, yet the letter contains a promise of them, so soon as necessary facts shall be known." [23] The whole was sooner and better done than he had expected.[24]

Occasionally it appeared that Jefferson doubted his own proposal to the ministers that the monopolies be broken up. His position tended, of course, to make him emphasize the mutual benefits to be derived from a freer system; but he realized that whatever France granted would be largely gratuitous, for his own nation had already given all in its power to insure the French alliance. The commercial rights of native citizens in the United States were but a short step above what had been allowed French traders there. Besides it was difficult to prevent opening the door to the English. Whatever he might gain in France, he knew that " the improvement of our commerce with France will be more advanced by negotiations at St. James than at Versailles." [25]

---

[21] Ibid.
[22] J. MSS., Oct. 22, 1786.
[23] Dip. Cor., vol. iii, p. 153.
[24] Jefferson to Adams, Oct. 27, 1786, J. MSS.
[25] J. MSS. This single observation is undated, but was probably made in 1786. John Bondfield, consular agent at Bordeaux, wrote

At the very time when counsel was needed, Jefferson had practically the whole burden of defending and furthering the foreign trade of the United States. Congress was almost inactive; Adams was ready to leave London; Jay was a half-year behind the progress in Europe. Otto had poisoned Vergennes' mind against Jay, reporting him biased against France and cold to all appeals.[26] The opinion was not justified, however, for in commenting on the Anglo-French commercial negotiations, then under way, Jay wrote Jefferson: " We hear the treaty between France and Britain will be concluded; if so, many consequences will doubtless result from it to us. . . . Some suspect that France and England will pursue similar systems of colonial commerce with us. Of this, however, some doubts remain on my mind. This country is still exceedingly out of humor with Britain, and every commercial privilege we have from France, beyond what Britain admits, strengthens our predilections for France." [27]

The treaty, however, gave to the English the privileges of the most favored European nation only, and any fear of concerted regulations for West Indian trade vanished.[28] France reserved the right to grant special favors to any nation not European, which could not well refer to any other than the United States. But each suggestion of admitting Americans to a wider participation in the trade of the French colonies roused a storm among the French merchants, to the point of endangering the ministry, and Jefferson abandoned his efforts to get such changes made, considering the situation desperate although not entirely hopeless.[29]

The trade between France and South Carolina gave promise of being the first to become reciprocal. To their principal

---

Jefferson that English vessels coming from America were getting advantages intended for Americans (Dec. 12, 1786, J. MSS.).

[26] French Transcripts, vol. xxxi, fol. 19, No. 32.

[27] Dip. Cor., vol. iii, p. 136.

[28] Martens, Recueil des Traites de L' Europe, vol. iv, p. 155.

[29] Jefferson to Izard, Nov. 18; Jefferson to Limozin, Dec. 22, 1787; Izard to Jefferson, April 4, 1787, all J. MSS. In official correspondence between Jefferson and the French ministry, this subject was mentioned but once in the year 1787.

item, rice, Jefferson gave a great deal of attention, in fact he wrote more letters and went to greater trouble to encourage this article than for any other during his entire ministerial residence in France. In the spring of 1787 he made a visit to the south of France, principally to try the effect of the mineral waters at Aix on his broken wrist, but also to see the Cathalans, father and son, about American commerce at Marseilles. While there he went on into Piedmont to learn by what methods the rice from that region was cleaned and how in general it excelled the Carolina variety. He found that the rice was from Lombardy, one hundred miles farther on; that the same machine was used in cleaning, but the grain was superior, enough so to account for the better reputation it had in French markets. Exportation of the grain for seed was prohibited, under penalty of death, but Jefferson managed to smuggle out a small amount to be sent for trial in South Carolina and Georgia. He felt somewhat conscience-stricken on taking off a month from his official duties for such a purpose, and vindicated himself to Jay. " The mass of our countrymen being interested in agriculture, I hope I do not err in supposing that in a time of profound peace as the present, to enable them to adopt their productions to the market, to point out markets for them, and endeavor to obtain favorable terms of reception, is within the line of my duty." [30]

Some of the samples sent to South Carolina were received while the legislature was in session. David Ramsay placed a parcel of it on the table in the House of Assembly,—exciting great interest and approbation among the planter members,— and caused Jefferson's letter to be printed in the official gazette.[31]

In order to get American rice to the Paris market he " had before endeavored to lead the depot of rice from Cowes to Honfleur, and hope to get it received there on such terms as may draw that branch of commerce from England to this

[30] Dip. Cor., vol. iii, p. 237.
[31] Ramsay to Jefferson, April 7, 1787, J. MSS.

country. It is an object of two hundred and fifty thousand guineas a year." [32] A Charleston firm, Brailsford and Morris, made a trial contract with Berard and Company of Paris, but the results were unsatisfactory. Later, Jefferson got still further samples from Egypt and from Cochin China, probably the first of these varieties to be tried in the United States. [33]

Returning to Paris from his journeying in the south, Jefferson began a new campaign on the extension of privileges. He found in his correspondence, an accumulation of complaints, alleging that the terms of the order of Bernis were not being observed by the Farmers-General, and these complaints were presented to Montmorin. [34] De Villedeuil made a vigorous response, insisting that the Farmers-General had been notified; and when the itemized accounts of purchases, with dates, amounts, prices, importers, and vessels, were demanded by Jefferson, they were given to him in such conclusive figures as to prove the suspicion of evasion by the Farmers-General was utterly wrong. [35]

The letter addressed to Montmorin reviewed the course of negotiations on tobacco up to July, 1787. Jefferson noted that the order of Bernis was never intended to be more than a temporary relief. The radical evil, he pointed out, would still exist, for there remained but one purchaser in France and his refusal would dampen every mercantile speculation. It was much to be desired that before the expiration of the order some measure might be devised which would bring this article into free commerce between the two nations. Had this been practicable at the time the Farm took it over, that system of collecting the revenue would probably never have been applied. Now that it was practicable, it seemed reasonable

---

[32] Dip. Cor., vol. iii, p. 262.

[33] Jefferson to S. Cathalan, Dec. 28, 1787; Jefferson to William Drayton, Jan. 13, 1788, both J. MSS.

[34] Who had succeeded Vergennes.

[35] De Villedeuil to Jefferson, July 2, 1787; N. Barrett to Jefferson, July 11, 1787; Berard et Cie to the Farmers-General, July 14, 1787; Joseph Fenwick to Jefferson, July 16, 1787; Jefferson to de la Boullaye, July 18, 1787; Jefferson to Montmorin, July 23, and Sept. 8, 1787; Bondfield to Jefferson, Oct. 12, 1787, all J. MSS.

to discontinue this method and to substitute some of those methods used for other imported articles on which a revenue was levied.

If the revenue can be secured, the interests of a few individuals will hardly be permitted to weigh against those of as many millions, equally subjects of His Majesty, and against those too of a nation allied to him by all the ties of a treaty, of interest and of affection. The privileges of the most favored nation have been mutually exchanged by treaty. But the production of other nations, which do not rival those of France, are suffered to be bought and sold freely within the kingdom. By prohibiting all His Majesty's subjects from dealing in tobacco except with a single company, one-third of the exports of the United States are rendered uncommerciable here.[36]

This production was so peculiarly American that the monopoly affected no other nation.

A relief from these shackles will form a memorable epoch in the commerce of the two nations. It will establish at once a great basis of exchange, serving like a point of union to draw to it other members of our commerce. Nature too has conveniently assorted our wants and our superfluities to each other. Each nation has exactly to spare the articles which the other wants. We have a surplus of rice, tobacco, furs, peltry, potash, lamp oils, timber, which France wants; she has a surplus of wines, brandies, esculent oils, fruits and manufactures of all kinds which we want. The governments have nothing to do but not to *hinder* their merchants from making the exchange. The difference of language, laws and customs will be some obstacle for a time; but the interest of the merchants will surmount them. A more serious obstacle is our debt to Great Britain. Yet since the treaty between this country and that, I should not despair of seing that debt paid in part with the productions of France if our produce can obtain here, a free course of exchange for them.[37]

As general as these arguments were, there was definite information behind them. Lists of American vessels entering and clearing from French harbors, the nature and amount of their cargoes had been supplied, at Jefferson's request, by the agents at the principal French ports. John Bondfield, at Bordeaux, was an especially valuable ally, not only for his statistics but for his keen evaluation of the connections be-

---

[36] Jefferson to Montmorin, July 23, 1787, J. MSS. This letter contains such a full expression of Jefferson's argument on commerce, that its ideas and even wording have not been much departed from here.

[37] Ibid.

tween the two countries. It was he who corroborated Jefferson's view that the basis of the French commercial system was wrong. He reported that the cargoes brought to Bordeaux from America were regularly paid for with specie or credit, four-fifths of which went to import goods from England or Scotland into the United States, leaving the American merchant no better off, financially, because prices were set by monopolists in France. The exportation of merchandise from Bordeaux to the United States had not amounted to more than three hundred thousand livres in three years.[38]

With the adjustment on tobacco as favorable as could be expected, so long as the Farmers-General controlled its reception in France, and the utmost done to enlarge the trade in rice, there remained the subject of whale oil. To push for improvement in the regulations on oils—whale oil and fish oils—required a greater stability in the ministry than could be discovered in the year of the Assembly of Notables, or, at least, until almost the end of that year. In the latter part of September, those interested in this business were startled by the appearance of an *arrêt* prohibiting the importation of whale oils and spermaceti, the product of foreign fisheries. Immediately the most important business facing the American ministers was whale oil and its protection. Another long review of an article of trade was written to Montmorin, and almost daily interviews were had with Lafayette and the ministers. Relying on favors not granted even to the most favored European nation, Jefferson insisted that the assurances given in the letters of preceding ministers amounted to a pledge, on which many merchants had staked their whole fortunes. " The importance," he wrote Montmorin, " of the subject to one of the principal members of our Union, induces me to attend with great anxiety the re-assurance from your Excellency, that no change has taken place in his Majesty's views on this subject; and that his dispositions to multiply rather than to diminish the combinations of interest between the two people, continue unaltered." [39]

---

[38] Bondfield to Jefferson, Sept. 11, Oct. 20, Nov. 30, 1787, and Jan. 15, 1788 all J. MSS.   [39] Dip. Cor., vol. iii, p. 320.

The serious depression to the business, and the fear that Lambert might be replaced by Necker, whose known antipathy to Americans would become ominous, hastened the agreement on an *arrêt* which disposed of all the commercial questions yet unsettled. During the time this *arrêt* was under consideration, Lambert had indicated that he would agree to a complete suppression of duties on products of the whale fisheries, but when this proposal was made to the council of ministers it was vigorously objected to, and for two months Jefferson exerted all of his persuasion to overcome the objections.[40]   As he wrote Jay:

I urged everything I could, in letters and in conferences to convince them that whale oil was an article which could bear no duty at all. That if the duty fell on the consumer, he would choose to buy vegetable oils; if on the fisherman, he would no longer live by his calling, remaining in his own country; and that if he quitted his own country, the circumstances of vicinity, sameness of language, laws, religion, and manners, and perhaps the ties of kindred would draw him to Nova Scotia, in spite of every encouragement which could be given at Dunkirk: and that thus those fishermen would be shifted out of a scale friendly to France, into one always hostile. Nothing however could prevail. It hung on this article alone for two months, during which we risked the total loss of the *arrêt* on the stability in office of M. Lambert; for if he had gone out, his successor, might be less favorable; and if Mr. Necker were the successor, we might lose the whole, as he never set any store by us, or the connection with us. About ten days ago it became universally believed that Mr. Lambert was to go out immediately. I therefore declined further insisting on the duties on whale oil as M. de Calonne had promised them; but with a reservation which may countenance our bringing on this matter again at a more favorable moment.[41]

The *arrêt* granted two special favors. One allowed the privilege of *entrepôt* in all the ports of France that were open to the commerce of her colonies. This amounted to practically the same thing as making all French ports free to Americans; for, while ships might be searched and cargoes had to be reported in the ports of *entrepôt*, and not in free ports, yet the continual, exasperating search of persons passing into the interior did not exist as between the free ports and the country. The other favor gave Americans the privileges

---

[40] J. T. Morse, Thomas Jefferson, p. 78.
[41] Dec. 31, 1787, J. MSS.

and advantages of native subjects in all the French possessions in Asia and in the " scales leading thereto," that is,
such islands or coasts on the routes to the Orient as were
already in France's possession, and more particularly those
which might be conquered in the threatened war with England. There was no hope of enjoying this advantage so long
as the French East India Company retained its monopoly,
for not even native subjects could enter French Asiatic ports
for purposes of commerce against its will, yet the disposition
to include the permission in an official document argued well
for future entrance of Americans into the French West
Indies.[42]

For nine months the regulation on whale oil continued in
force without interruption. Then, the new season having
glutted the French market with British oils, the demands of
their fishermen led the ministers to order that all whale oil
and spermaceti from foreign fisheries should be excluded from
France.[43] This sudden blow gave every appearance of wiping
out at a single stroke all of Jefferson's labors for the industry
during three years. It called for a test between the skill and
resources of the diplomat, the strength of the connection
between the nations, and the influence of the friends of the
United States, on the one side, and the weight of the demands
of French industry, the power of the monopoly principle, and
the fears of an unstable ministry, on the other.

The decision to exempt the United States from this order
was reached after eight weeks of debate between Jefferson
and the ministry. Besides letters and conferences, Jefferson
prepared especially for this case a printed pamphlet which
reviewed the entire transaction and the arguments he had
previously advanced. To the reader of this pamphlet, it
seems clear that the main reliances and his strongest points
are his insistence that bad faith would be shown if all former

---

[42] For a criticism of this *arrêt*, see a letter from Limozin to
Franklin, Jan. 26, 1788, Dip. Cor., vol. ii, p. 90; Jay to Lafayette,
April 26, 1788, ibid., vol. i, p. 456.
[43] A copy of the *arrêt* is in the Manuscripts, Sept. 28, 1788.

assurances of ministers, the *arrêts*, the careful reviewing of the complete range of trade and the matured conclusions thereon, should at a moment's notice be wiped out, and stability be replaced by mere expediency, and the expense to France of maintaining her fisheries. When the exemption was granted, the United States stood on a better footing than ever, since the products of her fisheries enjoyed with those of France, the benefits of the monopoly of supply.[44]

Just before the end of the year 1788 there was a further inducement to American shippers in the bounty put on wheat and flour. The scarcity of food stuffs, particularly in Paris, was the cause. The information was furnished by Necker and was passed on by Jefferson to Jay, with instructions to exporters in the United States on proving the American origin of their goods. This was published in American newspapers and came eventually to the notice of Mirabeau, who, in the States General, accused Jefferson of conspiring with American merchants to make capital of confidential advices. Under Jefferson's demand, Mirabeau later acknowledged his error and retracted the statement, while Jefferson used the occasion to urge on Montmorin the opportuneness of importing salted provisions from the United States and relieving the government of its heavy expense in doling out bread to the people. At the same time, and for the duration of the food shortage, the West India ports remained open to American vessels.[45]

According to notes in his manuscripts, Jefferson estimated that there were imported into France from the United States, in 1789, 140,959 barrels of flour; 3,664,576 bushels of wheat; and 12,340,000 pounds of rice. Vessels coming from the

---

[44] Jefferson to Montmorin, Oct. 23; to Limozin, Nov. 12; to Cathalan, Nov. 25; "Observations on Whale Fishery," November (date not given), all 1788, all J. MSS.; Dip. Cor., vol. iv, p. 6. The exemption was provisional only. Jefferson to Adams, Jan. 14, 1789, J. MSS.

[45] Dip. Cor., vol. iv, pp. 36, 107, 148; Jefferson to Limozin, Dec. 3, 1788; to Lafayette, June 12, 1789, July 6 and 7, 1789; to Necker, July 8; to Cavalier, July 27; to Robert Crew, Sept. 10; to John Mason, Sept. 16, 1789, all J. MSS.

United States to French ports in this year included 13 French, 43 English, and 163 American; the tonnage of American vessels was 19,173 in 1788, and 24,173 in 1789. Exports to France in 1788 were valued at $1,384,246; to French possessions in America, $3,284,656; and from them, $155,136 and $1,913,212, respectively. In this trade American tonnage was approximately ten times that of the French.

CHAPTER IV

THE CONSULAR CONVENTION

Among the American privateers outfitted in France during the Revolutionary War, was the " Alliance." A part of her supplies was furnished by the firm of Schweighauser and Dobrée. This firm laid its bills and vouchers before Barclay who pronounced them legitimate and exact, but payment on them was refused by Franklin because no audit had been made by Joshua Johnson, commissioned by Congress in 1781 to attend to it. This duty was transferred to Jefferson by Congressional order of October 16, 1786, and he began at once to follow it up. He found that a partner in the firm, Puchelberg, had attached a consignment of arms intended for the government of the United States, and had lodged them in a warehouse at Nantes. Jefferson made an inventory of the entire lot, finding 50,000 gun-locks, 30,000 bayonets, thirty cases of arms, and twenty-two cases of sabres, all badly rusted from inundation in a flood. He believed there might be legal difficulties attending their removal, and so referred to Congress for directions.[1]

This business regularly belonged to Barclay, but when he returned to France from the Moroccan mission he became involved with his creditors, so deeply in fact, that he felt obliged to escape the officers at Bordeaux by flight at night. From Lorient he took passage to the United States, leaving the dispute to be settled by Jefferson, although he, Franklin, and Lee had possessed all the information.[2]

Jefferson appealed to Schweighauser and Dobrée to refer

---

[1] Jefferson to Jay, Aug. 11, 1786; Barclay to Jefferson, July 16, 1787; Jefferson to Barclay, Aug. 3, and to the Commissioners of the Treasury, Aug. 9, 1787, all J. MSS.

[2] Dip. Cor., vol. iii, p. 266; Jefferson to Barclay, June 19, July 4 and 17, 1787, J. MSS. Copy of the "*Journal de Guienne*" for July 17, 1787, describing Barclay's case, is in the J. MSS. He was arrested once but released under consular immunity (Jefferson to Adams, July 23, J. MSS.).

the question to the arbitration of qualified neutrals, as could be found among the Dutch refugees then in Paris, but it was refused by Puchelberg. It was upon this refusal that Jefferson called into action a rule of international law, and put the responsibility for decision on the French court. Writing Montmorin, September 11, 1788, he said:

I presume it to be well settled in practice that the property of one sovereign is not permitted to be seized within the dominions of another; and that this practice is founded not only in mutual respect but in mutual utility. To what the contrary practice would lead is evident in the present case, wherein military stores have been stopped in the course of a war in which our greatest difficulties proceeded from the want of military stores; in their letter too they make a merit of not having seized one of our ships of war, and certainly the principle which admits the seizure of arms, would admit that of a whole fleet, and would often furnish an enemy the easiest means of defeating an expedition.[3]

The required promise for protection of the rights of the United States was given. Delivery of the arms was, however, delayed by conflict of opinion in the ministry, beyond the time of Jefferson's departure for America.[4]

Affairs of this nature as well as constant need for accommodation of American trade in the ports of France signified the need for a consular convention. By an act of January 25, 1782, Congress gave Franklin both a commission and a scheme for renewing a previous negotiation on such a convention, but when his results were presented, Jay attacked them so severely that Congress rejected the entire transaction.[5] A temporizing policy followed, during which the representatives in Europe, Barclay particularly, were instructed to manage consular matters, or to appoint Americans settled at the various ports to act as consuls. Jay was irritated and handicapped. The business of his office experienced " unseasonable delays and successive obstacles." More than ever he was convinced that the form of our government was wrong,

---

[3] J. MSS.
[4] Dip. Cor., vol. iii, p. 463; Jefferson to Reyneval, April 17; and to Jay, May 12, 1789, J. MSS.
[5] For the scheme and instructions, see Sec. Jour., vol. iii, p. 66. Jay's report is in Dip. Cor., vol. iii, pp. 159-185.

having as it did, three branches in one and that one constantly changing its membership, without checks from other branches.[6]

The basis for the authority of consuls in this inter-regnum was explained in a letter to Carmichael, in which Jefferson wrote:

> You intimate the expediency of the mutual appointment of consuls between Denmark and us. But our particular constitution occasions a difficulty. You know that a consul is the creature of a convention altogether; that without this he must be unknown and his jurisdiction unacknowledged by the laws of the country in which he is placed. The will of the sovereign in most countries can give him a jurisdiction by a simple order. With us, the Confederation admitting Congress to make treaties with foreign powers, they can by treaty or convention provide for the admission and jurisdiction of consuls, and the Confederation and whatever is done under it being paramount to the laws of the states, this establishes the power of the consuls. But without a convention, the laws of the states cannot take any notice of a consul, nor permit him to exercise any jurisdiction. In the case of Temple the consul from England therefore, Congress could only say he should have such powers as the law of nations and the laws of the states admitted. But none of the states having passed laws but for nations in alliance with us, Temple can exercise no jurisdiction nor authority.[7]

The merits of stable arrangements finally appeared convincing to Congress. Instructions were sent to Jefferson, October 3, 1786, to use the original scheme that had been used for governing Franklin's negotiation, a draft that was acknowledged to be far from perfect but from which he was not to recede. Moreover, the negotiation was to be limited to the points objected to by Jay's original report.[8] This plan was not satisfactory to the minister. He asked for revised instructions, without reference to the scheme, intimating that inasmuch as the United States was binding itself to a new institution, a procedure should be followed that kept no traces of earlier dissatisfaction. However the convention might be arranged, the United States would, he believed, be in worse

[6] Ibid., vol. iii, p. 71; Jefferson to Gen. Warren, Feb. 8; to Bondfield, Aug. 3, 1786, J. MSS. Otto reported to Vergennes that Rufus King was causing the delay in Congress (French Trans, vol. xxxi-B, fol. 320, No. 49).
[7] Aug. 22, 1786, J. MSS.
[8] Dip. Cor., vol. iii, p. 72.

situation than before, if only because of granting away a part of her jurisdiction.[9] But his complaint was not effective. On July 27, 1787, Congress gave him full powers to proceed, on the plan outlined, with a twelve-year limit, and a virtual promise to ratify what he should submit.

Before this negotiation was actually begun, and upon Barclay's appeal for protection against his creditors, as a diplomatic character, the question of the immunity of consuls arose. Montmorin assured Jefferson that they had no such privilege in case of debt. So far as Barclay was minister to Morocco, that would give him the status he desired; but his long stay at Bordeaux had terminated such character. No country in Europe aside from France took notice of the character of a minister *en passage* between two other nations, Montmorin observed, and France did not permit a minister to her court to depart without paying his debts,—a practice that Jefferson believed could not be justified by the law of nations.[10] But he did agree that consuls should not enjoy exemption from arrest. This opinion became Jay's, too, and was recommended by him to Congress as a settled policy.[11]

Although there were constant demands for the adjustment of minor business and commercial affairs, normally belonging to the office of consuls, no vigorous action on the convention was undertaken for a year and a half from the date of the commission to Jefferson in the fall of 1786. His delay was due to several causes. First, the United States had no treaties of amity and commerce except those on the most favored nation principle; any extension of privileges was therefore necessarily opened to many nations,—not merely to France. In the second place, he preferred to allow a lapse of time long enough to insure forgetfulness of Franklin's unsuccessful negotiation. And, finally, he did not mean to risk forcing on the ministers too many matters of business, especially when he was urging more favorable regulations for the admission

---

[9] Jefferson to Jay, Jan. 9, 1787, J. MSS.

[10] Jefferson to Barclay, July 4, 1787, ibid.

[11] Dip. Cor., vol. iii, p. 260.

of American goods into France. So that it was in mid-summer of 1788 when he laid before Montmorin the Congressional scheme with the proposed changes. At the same time he explained the American attitude toward consuls. They were, he said, little and unfavorably known; the considerable commerce of the United States was carried on without a consul in any port and yet there was no complaint, except from those who wanted appointments as consuls. It would be difficult for his nation to overcome some legal obstacles; the laws were much the same as in England, in whose ports consuls had no powers.[12]

The basis being established, the French answered with a counter-proposal, and during the succeeding five months, June 20 to November 14, the opposing views were brought into harmony in the final convention as signed. The discussions over disputed points revolved about differences between the French and American systems of jurisprudence rather than the opinions of the negotiators, except in respect to some points of international law. On these Jefferson insisted, successfully, on the adoption of the American view. The main issues were soon reduced to these four questions:

1. Shall consuls and others attached to their offices retain personal immunities?
2. Shall navigation codes of each nation be established in the territories of the other?
3. Must a consul be present in every case of visit or arrest by local officials on board the vessels of his nation, whether vessels of commerce or of war?
4. Shall the captain's word, or the ship's roll, be conclusive evidence as to the presence of any person sought on board the ship?[13]

On the first of these the French proposal was to allow to consuls and others attached to the consulates, personal im-

---

[12] Jefferson to Montmorin, June 20, 1788, J. MSS. In the Manuscripts under the same date is a copy of the proposed convention. The parts of the old scheme intended to be omitted are boxed with red lines. All additions are written in with red pencil.
[13] Jefferson to Reyneval, Sept. 16, 1788, J. MSS.

munity from the laws of the land except in cases of crime
or of debt.   To this Jefferson objected on two grounds.
First, it would create a character new to international rela-
tionships, belonging neither to the class of persons subject
to the laws of the land, nor to that subject only to the laws
of nations.   The obligations and privileges of these classes
were so well known and agreed upon that no dispute could
arise over them, but a middle group would be subject to no
clear rules, a source of continual questioning and disagreement.   Secondly, the exemption of subordinates in the
consulates would unnecessarily swell the number of persons
unamenable to the law, not required to protect them in their
duties, and sufficiently covered in the phrase,—" exempting
them from all personal services,"—inserted in another part of
the convention.   This reasoning prevailed in the final draft,
and all exemptions were enumerated.[14]

The second point in dispute was embodied in the eighth
article of the French proposal, which would allow consuls
civil jurisdiction on board their national vessels, power to
enforce ordinances relative to navigation, and the right to go
on board for these purposes at any time.   To the first and
third of these no objection could be raised, but the second
could not be agreed to:

Because it establishes a whole code at once, the contents of which
are unknown to the party within whose territory it is to be executed.
When each concedes to the other a civil jurisdiction within its own
ports, it knows the extent of its concession; but when it permits
the enforcement of all the navigation laws of the other, in a lump,
it does not know what it concedes. They may include a criminal
jurisdiction, they may be contrary to bills of rights; or, if not so
at present, they may be hereafter. It is surely prudent and honorable
for us to stipulate to each other only what we know we can execute.
But we do not know we can execute if we do not know what we
stipulate.[15]

The wording of the article later agreed upon was arranged
to meet this objection.

In providing against the desertion of members of a crew,
and to insure their return, there was no disagreement over

---

[14] Dip. Cor., vol. iii, pp. 483, 498.
[15] Ibid., p. 478.

giving a full grant of power to consuls. But the French view that this power should extend to " other persons " beyond the regularly defined crew, and that the ship's roll should be conclusive evidence as to who did or did not belong to the ship, seemed to Jefferson to carry the authority too far. " A master of a ship, for instance," he observed, " inserting in his roll the name of a citizen of the United States, who had never seen his ship, that citizen must be delivered to him, if these words were to remain. It is not probable indeed, that the master of a ship would be so indiscreet, but, neither is it proper to rest personal liberty on the discretion of a master of a ship." [16]

Whether the arrest of persons accused of crime, on board a vessel of the consul's nation, should be made only in the presence of the consul occasioned a long argument. It involved, of course, the fear that prejudice against foreigners might prompt the local magistrates to make false arrests, detain vessels in port beyond reason, and interfere with the general interests of commerce, whereas protection of those interests was the very purpose for which consuls were exchanged. This proposition was new to the American view. Whatever clogged the free course of national jurisdiction was undesirable to a legalist like Jefferson. It would, in his opinion, substitute the disposition or the bias of a consul for the initial steps of officers of the law. The distance of the consul from the scene, the pressure of his business at the moment, his personal activity and good faith, instead of justice and settled methods of executing it, would govern cases, no matter how flagrant, involving the commercial class of his country. The conclusion of the argument was that in the convention the requirement for personal attendance of consuls in these cases was waived in favor of adequate notice to them by judges of the country.

Another contest arose over the question of arrest of criminals on board war ships. The French contention was that the civil and military authorities should not exercise any jurisdiction whatsoever on the warship of a friendly nation. The

[16] Ibid., p. 487.

captain's word as to the presence of offenders was final. In so far as this would make the ports of the two countries extra-territorial, it induced the same opposition as the preceding proposal. As Jefferson reasoned:

The Convention of the neutral powers in the late war, made the captain's word conclusive evidence, that no contraband goods were on board the vessels under his convoy; but this in cases arising on the high seas. The sea belongs to no nation. No nation, therefore, has a natural right to search the ships of another on the high seas. The contrary practice has been an abuse, and the abandonment of it is a reformation of that abuse, a re-establishment of natural right. But the ports of a nation are a part of its territory. They are often within the body of a town, and an immunity from the restraint of law granted to strangers within the port, would be as productive of disorder, as if granted to those in the town, or in the country. All judges, civil and criminal, derive their authority from the Sovereign of the country wherein they act. For the encouragement of commerce, it is become usual to permit, by Conventions, foreign merchants of the same country to refer their disputes to a judge of their own. But in criminal cases, in cases which interest members of their own, or any other state, or the state itself, it is apprehended not to be the practice for the nation to part with its authority, and that neither order nor justice would be promoted by it. Particularly to leave to the discretion of a captain, whether his ship shall be an asylum for fugitive debtors, whether the disorders or crimes committed by his sailors, or by others, taking refuge in his ship, should be punished or not, cannot be a means of encouraging the commerce between two nations, nor promote the interest or honor of either. Nor has the impunity any relation to the function of a consul, which are the sole object of the present Convention.[17]

This matter was settled by being omitted from the Convention, although it may be interpreted as leaving warships subject to action of the territorial authorities since the eleventh article provided that *any* vessel might be visited and arrests made thereon.

The significance of this Convention is not merely that it was the first to be agreed to by the United States, but that it was constructed in such form as to give maximum protection to the national interests. Municipal and international law were harmonized so far as possible, and the American conceptions yielded as little as possible. Jefferson's knowledge of the law, and his sincere devotion to its unimpaired maintenance, caused him to reach in this negotiation the highest point of technical service that he performed for the United States during his mission to France.

---

[17] Ibid.

CHAPTER V

TREATIES OBSTRUCTED

The zeal of the American ministers in Europe for treaties with the nations named in their original instructions cooled considerably after Franklin's departure. The glow of enthusiasm for general connections was modified by experience into a calmer realization of the specific problems presented in each treaty projected. It is often assumed that the reasons for the small number of treaties actually signed by the United States, from the end of the Revolutionary War to Jay's Treaty, may be generalized into the conclusion that her governmental ineffectiveness and her poor financial condition made her international status hopeless and diplomatic relations with her uninviting. While this view can not be waived aside entirely, yet it is true that the negotiations which were begun but not completed hinged on more particular considerations,—they were, in fact, as often abandoned by American representatives as by European. Only in the case of Portugal was there any anxiety or any approach toward supplication shown.

In the case of the central European powers, the procrastination of Congress was the main cause of the failure to secure treaties. The progress of the Prussian negotiation awakened fresh interest on the part of the Empire. The imperial ambassador at Paris, in a conversation with Jefferson early in 1786, expressed surprise that Jefferson did not know that an answer had been returned to Franklin's overtures, and hastened to furnish a copy of it. While the project concerned the Austrian Netherlands only, Jefferson favored such a negotiation. Writing Gerry in May, 1786, he said:

The Emperor is now pressing a treaty with us. In a commercial view, I doubt whether it is desirable: but in a political one I believe it is. He is now undoubtedly the second power in Europe, and on the death of the King of Prussia he becomes the first character. An alliance with him will give us respectability in Europe, which we have occasion for. Besides he will be at the head of the

66

second grand confederacy of Europe, and may at any time serve us with the powers constituting that.[1]

But Jefferson's power for undertaking this kind of business had expired, and although he called it to the attention of Congress several times, it was not renewed.[2]

A potential treaty with Denmark was defeated by trouble between John Paul Jones and that government. During the Revolutionary War he had carried three prizes into Bergen; they were restored to the British by order of the Danish officials, an action which brought on a course of diplomatic exchanges. This affair had not been settled when Jefferson arrived in France, and as Adams would take no responsibility in it, he was obliged to follow it up. Franklin had refused an offer of ten thousand pounds for settlement. Adopting the same attitude, Jefferson reviewed the case with Baron Blome, Danish minister at Paris, and advised him that "Commodore" Jones was being sent to Copenhagen to determine the issue.[3] This was without authorization of Congress, except for approval of the agent; but, directly after this, official sanction was given. The ground that it was a breach of international law was abandoned, and it was made a question of diplomacy.[4]

The way was prepared for Admiral Jones by a letter to Count Bernstorff, Danish Minister for Foreign Affairs, asking that full restitution of the value of the prizes be made, and one to Montmorin urging his help, since about half of the money would go to French subjects.[5] Jones was instructed to have payments made to the bankers of Denmark in Amsterdam or in Paris. When he arrived at Copenhagen, he addressed a note to Bernstorff, emphasizing the promise of

[1] May 7, 1786; Jefferson to Adams, Jan. 12, 1786, two of the same date, J. MSS.
[2] Dip. Cor., vol. iii, pp. 138, 316; Jefferson to Dumas, Nov. 14, and to Jay, Dec. 21, 1787, J. MSS.
[3] Adams to Jefferson, Nov. 4, 1785, and July 17, 1786; Jefferson to Baron Blome, Aug. 18, 1786, J. MSS.
[4] Edward Carrington to Jefferson, Nov. 10, 1787, J. MSS.
[5] Dip. Cor., vol. iii, p. 360; Jefferson to Montmorin, Jan. 26, 1788, J. MSS.

"prompt and explicit decision"; after a week's wait without a reply, he wrote again, impatient, since nine years from the event must, he insisted, have given time for concluding it. Waiting still another week, he wrote one of the sharpest demands to be found in diplomatic correspondence; upon which he had the satisfaction of learning the reasons for the procrastination. His powers, he was told, were insufficient; the Danish court wished to see the outcome of the constitutional convention in the United States; besides, the business was started in Paris and should be finished there.[6] Within a month he had given up the mission and was in command of the naval forces of the empress of Russia.

Bernstorff connected the settlement of the prize money with the adoption of a commercial treaty with the United States, and so informed Jefferson. This subterfuge was irritating. There was no logical connection between the two. Moreover, it was unfair to make American seamen await so uncertain an event, and Jefferson pushed their claims with such resources as he could command.[7] But the Danish ministers hid behind their excuse; Jefferson could obtain no answer, and he left France without a settlement of the prize money, which, of necessity, precluded any preliminary negotiation on the treaty.

The initial steps on a treaty with Portugal were taken by Adams in London, in the fall of 1785. The Chevalier de Pinto had been authorized to begin on such preliminaries, and the two men had discussed the chief issues in the commerce of their nations,—the free introduction of flour from the United States into the port of Lisbon, the extent to which Americans would be allowed to trade in Portuguese colonies, and the effects of the proposed navigation act in the United States.[8] At about the same time, Jefferson made overtures to the Portuguese minister at Paris. In his manuscripts, dated only "1786," is the copy of a project for a treaty, based on the

---

[6] Dip. Cor., vol. iii, p. 391.
[7] Jefferson to Bernstorff June 19, 1788, ibid., p. 414; to Jay, May 4, 1788, ibid., p. 387; to M. de Chamillard, June 29, 1788, to John Paul Jones, Mar. 23, 1789, J. MSS.
[8] Adams to Jefferson, Nov. 5, 1785, J. MSS.

most favored nation plan and containing some of the provisions written into the treaty with Prussia. His accom-
panying " observations " provide an index to his views, particularly on the regulation of contraband. He believed that
provisions should not be included in that category; contraband
was only a relic and not a logical rule, for every nation could
produce the articles it covered and the greatest security against
its possible abuse lay in the example of nations, not in their
force. The most favored nation principle in this treaty would,
he thought, be defeated by Portugal's commercial regulations,
for, under conditions of climate, the Russians and Dutch
would eliminate competition by the United States.

Another page of notes, placed with these, and with the
same date, intimates that a letter was contemplated, probably
to Jay, but if written, it has been lost. In part it reads:
" Would it not be prudent to send a minister to Portugal.
Our commerce with that country is very important, perhaps
more so than that of any country in Europe. It is possible
too that they might permit our whaling vessels to refresh in
Brazil, or give some other indulgences in America, the lethar-
gic character of their ambassador here gives a very unhopeful
aspect to a treaty on this ground." But Adams was making
progress. In the spring of 1786, he called Jefferson to London
where conferences with Pinto were drawn out over seven
weeks and a treaty agreed to. Adams and Jefferson signed it,
but at the last moment, Pinto disclosed the fact that he could
not sign without submitting the draft to his court.[9] It contained the most favored nation clause but did not permit
the admission of flour, nor did it give any privileges in the
American possessions of Portugal.

The courier sent by the Chevalier de Pinto to carry the
copy of the agreement to his government missed the boat at
Falmouth and was delayed for a month. The ensuing unfortunate turn against the treaty in Portugal was accounted for
by Adams and Jefferson by this incident; but it is hardly to
be doubted that Carmichael estimated the reasons more clearly

[9] Dip. Cor., vol. iii, p. 4; Jefferson to Jay, April 23, 1786, J. MSS.

when he ascribed the difficulty to the renewal of close relations
between England and Portugal.[10]   But the announcement of
the Portuguese queen that she had ordered her warships to
protect American merchant vessels against the pirates led
Congress to send Colonel W. S. Smith to Lisbon with an
expression of thanks, and he informed Jefferson of what he
could learn about the treaty.   The delay, he was told, was
caused by Pinto's long absence and his lack of appreciation
of the policies of his court.   The treaty would be scrutinized
and a counter-project returned; but it was distasteful to them
to treat at London.   An exchange of resident ministers would
remove some bad feeling.[11]

This condition was still unremedied when Jefferson left
for America.   After he came into the State Department it
was felt that a confidential agent should be sent to give
Carmichael " a more intimate account of affairs," since he
had been so long out of touch, and David Humphreys was
selected for the purpose.   As a measure of economy he was
made *chargé d'affaires* at Lisbon, but this grade was so unsat-
factory to de Pinto, now Minister for Foreign Affairs in
Portugal, that he was not acknowledged.[12]   His explanation
of the insufficiency of Congress' appropriation for a higher
rank was not acceptable; hence Jefferson "nominated" him
as minister resident and Congress confirmed the choice.

The last move during Jefferson's tenure of his secretary's
post was to instruct Humphreys on bringing pressure for
admission of American flour into Portugal.   As he wrote:

It seems then that so far from giving new liberties to our corn
trade, Portugal contemplates the prohibition of it, by giving that
trade exclusively to Naples.   What would she say should we give
our wine trade exclusively to France and Spain?   It is well known
that far the greatest proportion of the wine we consume is from
Portugal and its dependencies, and it must be foreseen that from the

[10] Adams to Jefferson, July 3, 1786, and Jan. 25, 1787, Dip. Cor.,
vol. iii, p. 126.
[11] Smith to Jefferson, Sept. 18, 1787, J. MSS.
[12] Humphreys to the Secretary of State, Nov. 30, 1790; Jefferson's
Report to the Senate, Feb. 18, 1791; and to the Secretary of the
Treasury, Mar. 12, 1791, J. MSS.

natural increase of population in these states, the demand will
become equal to the uttermost abilities of Portugal to supply, even
when her last foot of land shall be put into culture.[13]

He believed this was cause enough to convince any wise
statesman that trade should be made reciprocal.

While he was visiting in the south of France, in the spring
of 1787, Jefferson received a mysterious caller at his hotel in
Nismes, who represented himself as a Brazilian patriot seeking
aid in the probable revolt of his country. The substance of
his plea was that Brazil, oppressed by the hated Portuguese,
was ready for a revolution but she feared the combination of
Spain with Portugal. Needing an ally, she turned naturally
to the United States, by whose example she was inspired.
Jefferson hastened to remind him of the friendliness between
the United States and Portugal; yet he admitted it was an
interesting suggestion, and gave some information about
getting men as officers. A similar proposal had been made
to him by a Mexican in Paris, somewhat earlier, but he was
suspicious in this case. He pointed out that it was no object
to the United States to give up present and certain advantages of good relations with Spain for future uncertain ones
with Mexico. His suspicions were made convictions when he
saw the Mexican at the Spanish embassy in Paris.[14]

Every one of the European treaty negotiations was left as
a legacy of half-finished business to Jefferson. Of them all,
only the English aggravated him more than the Spanish.
Although Jay, as Secretary for Foreign Affairs under the
Confederation, had been responsible for preventing a clash
with Spain over the troublesome questions of the Indians and
the navigation of the Mississippi, he had not achieved any
positive results nor established any desirable principles for
dealing with Spain in America. But Jefferson had formed
convictions on this phase of our foreign relations while he
was in France, and his views pervaded the diplomacy of the
United States for more than a century. On January 25,

---

[13] Jefferson to Humphreys, Nov. 7, 1792, J. MSS.
[14] Dip. Cor., vol. iii, p. 239.

1786, he wrote a letter to Alexander Stuart in which he revealed his opinion that both Americas should be peopled from the United States. " We should take care too not to think it for the interest of that great continent to press too soon on the Spaniards. Those countries cannot be in better hands. My fear is that they are too feeble to hold them till our population can be sufficiently advanced to gain it from them piece by piece. The navigation of the Mississippi we must have. This is all we are as yet ready to receive." [15]

The information Jefferson received from Madrid was contained in the letters of Carmichael. Although he was markedly remiss in sending news to Congress, Carmichael wrote frequently to Jefferson, sometimes on matters of moment and again merely on his personal grievances.[16] As Jefferson stated, confidentially, to Madison:

I have now a constant correspondence with him, and find him a little hypochondriac and discontented. He possesses very good understanding, tho' not of the first order. I have had great opportunities of searching into his character, and have availed myself of them. Many persons of different nations, coming from Madrid to Paris, all speak of him as in high esteem, and I think it certain that he has more of the Count de Florida Blanca's friendship, than any diplomatic character at that court. As long as this minister is in office, Carmichael can do more than any other person who could be sent there.[17]

Carmichael was so little known in the United States and so inattentive to Congress, that he was ignored. Jay and the Spanish agent at New York, Gardoqui, were given free rein in disposing of the questions of the use of the Mississippi and the southern boundary. But when it appeared to members of Congress that no headway was being made, Monroe moved to take the business out of Jay's hands and put it under control of a congressional committee. This was only defeated because it was felt that they had too far committed themselves, and because of the threat of a treaty between

---

[15] J. MSS.
[16] A. C. McLaughlin, Report on the Diplomatic Archives of the Department of State, 1789-1840, p. 12; Carmichael to Jefferson, Dec. 17, 1785, J. MSS., is a sample of Carmichael's discontent.
[17] Writings, vol. v, p. 258; W. C. Ford, The United States and Spain in 1790, p. 17.

Spain and England. The proposition stood on the ground of closing the river for thirty years in consideration of Spain's admitting vessels and goods of the United States into her ports on an equal footing with those of her own subjects, and reciprocally for the United States.[18] Monroe's opposition to this was concurred in by Jefferson who agreed that no amity could be pretended to so long as the right to the Mississippi was denied by Spain. Madison endeavored to induce Congress to send Jefferson to Madrid to carry on the negotiations and to enter into a general commercial arrangement, but Jay succeeded in blocking the adoption of this plan, although it was apparent that further discussions with Gardoqui were futile.[19]

It was rather on the basis of policy than from compatibility between the two nations that Jefferson settled his conviction on the necessity of peaceful relations. Carmichael reported that he had written promises " that America shall be treated as the most favored nation, until a commercial treaty fixes the footing on which we are to be with this country." In his answer, Jefferson said : " I cannot help suspecting the Spanish squadron to be gone to South America, and that some disturbances have been excited there by the British. The Court of Madrid may suppose we would not see this with an unwilling eye. This may be true as to the uninformed part of our people; but those who look into futurity farther than the present moment or age, and who combine well what is, with what is to be, must see that our interests well understood, and our wishes are that Spain shall (not forever) but, very long retain her possessions in that quarter; and that her views and ours must, in a good degree, and for a long time concur." [20] Yet he did not underestimate the feelings of the westerners in the United States. " I never had any interest Westward of the Alleghaney," he wrote Madison, " and I

---

[18] Monroe to Jefferson, June 16, and Jefferson to Monroe, Aug. 11, 1786, J. MSS.

[19] Sec. Jour., vol. iv, p. 338; Jefferson to Madison, June 20, 1787, Writings, vol. v, p. 283.

[20] Dip. Cor., vol. iii, p. 409; Carmichael to Jefferson, April 14, 1788, J. MSS.

never will have any. But I have had great opportunities of knowing the character of the people who inhabit that country, and I will venture to say that the act which abandons the navigation of the Mississippi is an act of separation between the Eastern and Western country." [21]

While Jefferson was Secretary of State, the points of issue with Spain were upon the opening of the Mississippi to navigation, the location of the southern boundary line, the adjustment of relations with the Indians who were located on or near the boundary, and the conclusion of a commercial treaty. Two Spanish envoys, Viar and Jaudenes, " resided near " Congress, at first as secret agents, later as *chargés d'affaires,* and it was through them that most of the business was conducted. This was practically compulsory so long as Carmichael remained untrusted, and apparently indifferent.

To give Carmichael such intimate appreciation of the policies of his country as a diplomat should have, and of which he complained he was not cognizant because he had been neglected by the home government, Jefferson wrote him several dispatches containing both the history and status of the several problems, and his own views on them, as head of the State Department. On the Indians, he recited the methods used by the United States to establish peace. The treaties fixing boundaries were satisfactory to all of the tribes except the Creeks, who had been invited to New York where a new agreement was reached. All went smoothly until a disturber, Bowles, created trouble. The Spaniards pretended to suppress him,[22] but they adopted his system, called assemblies of the Indians and got them to throw off their treaty obligations to the United States. In thus assuming a frontier before settlement, Spain's officials were putting the onus of inciting the Indians on the United States, and making peaceful relations impossible. " That if we are to repel the attacks of the Creeks, on ourselves, it will disturb our peace with Spain.

[21] Jan. 30, 1787, Writings, vol. v, p. 254.
[22] Washington told Jefferson that the arrest of Bowles was a farce, and that he was then living in Madrid (Washington to Jefferson, Aug. 23, 1792, J. MSS.).

That if we will not fold our arms and let them butcher us
without restitution, Spain will consider it a cause of war."
This condition was so serious that the President wished it to
be taken over the heads of Viar and Jaudenes, directly to the
Spanish court.

> If we are disappointed in this appeal, if we are to be forced into
> a contrary order of things, our mind is made up. We shall meet it
> with firmness. The necessity of our position, will supercede all
> appeal to calculation, now, as it has done heretofore, we confide in
> our own strength, without boasting of it; we respect that of others,
> without fearing it. If we cannot otherwise prevail on the Creeks
> to discontinue their depredations, we will attack them in force. If
> Spain chuses to consider our self-defense against savage-butchering
> as a cause of war to her, we must meet her also in war, with regret,
> but without fear; and we shall be happier to the last moment to
> repair with her to the tribunal of Peace and Reason.[23]

It was an auspicious moment to talk war, for Spain was then
involved in the Nootka Sound controversy with England.[24]
The resulting developments brought the two nations almost
to war. It is not too much to say that if Viar and Jaudenes
had been fully authorized representatives of Spain, and had
not been regularly ignored, they would have led the negotiations into hostilities. For more than three years they per-
sisted in nagging and insulting the government of the United
States with accounts of intrigues and unworthy schemes set
on foot by American envoys among the Indian tribes, until
no other interpretation but that of deep maliciousness and
enmity toward Spain could be placed on the policy of Washington's administration. The chief offender, these two said,
was governor Blount, who had even bribed several chiefs with
silver medals bearing the effigy of Washington and the legend,
" Friendship and Trade without End." [25]

Not without considerable consequences was the monopoly on
commerce with the Creek nation given to Colonel McGillivray.
In an opinion on this subject, Jefferson held that the Creeks
were within their rights if they wished to assent to a treaty

---

[23] Jefferson to Carmichael, June 30, 1790, J. MSS.
[24] Ford, p. 43.
[25] De Viar and Jaudenes to Jefferson, May 25, Aug. 10, Oct. 29,
1792, and June 18, 1793, J. MSS.

embodying the official agreement between the President and McGillivray that goods should be admitted duty free, and that a limited number of licenses should be sent to McGillivray, in blank, for him to fill in. The question as to whether this privilege could be withdrawn by an act of Congress led Jefferson into an " observation " on the place of treaties in American law. " A treaty made by the President with the concurrence of two-thirds of the Senate, is a law of the land, and a law of superior order, because it not only repeals past laws, but cannot itself be repealed by future ones." In the manuscripts, at this point, is a footnote in darker ink, with no new date but evidently of a later day,[26] reading: " unless with the consent or default of the other contracting party, it may well be doubted too, & perhaps denied that the treaty power can control a law, the question here proposed was then of the 1st impression, subsequent investigations have proved that the contrary position is the more general truth, the treaty then will legally control the duty-act, and the act for licensing traders, in this particular instance." [27]

James Seagrove, the temporary deputy of the United States to the Creeks, convinced Washington of the machinations of the Spaniards along the West Florida boundary, where they were trying to prevent the running of the boundary between the United States and the Creeks. The report implicated McGillivray. Washington was so much worried that he wrote Jefferson to ask him to make a strong statement to the Spanish *chargés.* He confided to Jefferson his belief that Spain was aided and abetted by England, and that both wished to retard the growth of the United States.[28] With another communication from Viar and Jaudenes, asserting that the United States was stirring up the Indians while Spain was trying to pacify them, and with ugly accusations in the newspapers charging the reverse, Washington called a cabinet meeting to decide on what recommendation, if any,

---

[26] It is so interpreted by Ford, in the Writings, vol. vi, p. 111.
[27] Ibid.; July 29, 1790, J. MSS.
[28] Washington to Jefferson (from Mt. Vernon), Oct. 31, 1792, J. MSS.

should be made to Congress, and what statement should be made to Spain. Jefferson argued for laying the question before both houses of Congress, since it might lead to war and some members would agree to war with Indian tribes but not with Spain. Moreover, he held that the whole should be referred for " negocian " to Madrid since that would postpone hostilities, would not put the territorial rights of the United States under doubt, and would avoid a rupture with Spain.[29]

This opinion was adopted by the cabinet. There are some indications, however, that it was Washington's anxiety rather than Jefferson's logic which settled this phase of diplomacy. Jefferson wrote the set of instructions to Short and Carmichael, but the President inspected them with unusual care, adding and striking out several key words.[30] In this document, after explaining Viar's and Jaudenes' objections to the Creek treaty, Jefferson said : " but besides that you already know the nullity of their pretended claim to the territory. They had themselves set the example of endeavoring to strengthen that claim by the treaty mentioned in the letter of the Baron de Carondelet,[31] and by the employment of an Agent among them,—the establishment of our boundary, committed to you, will of course remove the grounds of all future pretence to interfere with the Indians within our territory and it was to such only that the treaty of New York stipulated protection; for we take for granted that Spain will be ready to agree to the principle that neither party has a right to stipulate protection or interference with the Indian nations inhabiting the territory of the other, but it is extremely material also with sincerity & good faith to patronize the peace of each other with the neighboring savages." [32]

Contiguity with East Florida was the source of another boundary question. This was extradition. It arose out of

[29] " Notes of a Cabinet meeting," Oct. 31, 1792, J. MSS.
[30] Nov. 3, 1792, J. MSS.
[31] Governor of Louisiana. The letter was enclosed in that of Viar and Jaudenes to Jefferson, Oct. 29, 1792, J. MSS.
[32] Jefferson to Short and Carmichael, Nov. 3, 1792, J. MSS.

the grievance on the American side that slaves escaping into
Florida were deemed free; and on the Spanish side that
criminals, of whatever nationality, found a refuge in Georgia.
Governor Pinckney, of South Carolina, referred to Washington for advice on the advisability of demanding the return
of fugitives by Governor Quesada, of East Florida. Upon the
President's request Jefferson outlined an answer, developing
the legal and diplomatic sides of extradition. It was, he
pointed out, a matter of treaty, and the causes for it were
specifically enumerated. Since the United States and Spain
had no convention, the demand could not logically be made,
or at least the refusal could give no offence. Besides, a convention would of necessity be reciprocal and the United States
might not always care to deliver fugitives from Florida, in
view of the small difference between criminals and victims of
tyrannical rule.[33] Four months later, on March 22, 1792,
Jefferson laid before the President the project of a convention
and his examination of the principles underlying it. It
would establish murder as the only unconditioned cause for
extradition, although such protection to society as required
the inclusion of other crimes should not be denied. Flight
after treason, forgery, crimes against property, and on account
of debt, were sufficiently punished by the exile they entailed.
The process of demand should be by application to a justice
of the Supreme Court or a district judge, and the order for
deportation should be issued only after indictment and proof
of guilt. Washington's only objection was that the time of
action was left indefinite.[34] This convention and its explanations were sent to Carmichael with instructions that they
were to apply only to those Spanish provinces bordering on
the United States.[35]

Two cases arose under this head while the convention was
being constructed. One was that of John Church who had

[33] Jefferson to the President, Nov. 17, 1791, J. MSS.
[34] " Project for a Convention and Heads of Consideration," March
22, 1792; Washington to Jefferson, March 25, 1792, J. MSS.; H. D.
Gilpin, Biographical Sketch of Thomas Jefferson, p. 293.
[35] Jefferson to Carmichael and Short, April 24, 1792, J. MSS.

lived for two years in Havana, working at a trade, and had been convicted and punished under the laws of Spain. There was no appeal to be made. " Having made himself a Spanish subject, we have no more right to inquire into that judgment than the court of Spain would have to do the same with respect to the criminals now in our jails." [36] The other was a complaint that the master of an American vessel in a harbor of San Domingo induced some negroes aboard under pretence of hiring them, and then carried them off and sold them as slaves in Georgia. Jefferson considered two questions on this case; first, whether the general government could take cognizance, and secondly, whether there was any law under which he could be punished. The answers caused a scrutiny of the constitutional law. The " general welfare " clause evoked an interpretation : " I suppose its meaning to be that Congress may collect taxes for the purpose of providing for the *general welfare,* in those cases, wherein the Constitution empowers them to act for the general welfare. To suppose that it was meant to give them a distinct and substantive power, to do *any act* which might tend to the *general welfare,* is to render all the enumerations useless, and to make their powers unlimited." [37] He found that it was not covered by the piracy clause, but the eleventh section of the Judiciary Act would fit, under " all offences cognizable under the authority of the United States, and not otherwise provided for." [38]

This last case and another of forcible recovery by several Georgians of their slaves, from Florida, prompted Jefferson to suggest that the President include in his annual message to Congress a tacit admission that American citizens had offended against peaceful relations with other nations, and a recommendation for legislation on infractions of international law.[39] When this was called to its attention, the Senate

[36] Jefferson to Samuel and Sheppard Church, April 24, 1792, J. MSS.

[37] Notes, October, 1792, J. MSS.

[38] Ibid.

[39] " Suggestion for part of president's message," Nov. 1, 1792, J. MSS.

required its judiciary committee to inquire into the facts. In his "memoranda" on this, Jefferson put forth several propositions for the consideration of the legislature. Neither of the cases was cognizable in the United States as a crime because committed outside her boundaries; the United States had no power to deliver up an offender, although damages might be recovered; the law of nations was by its character a part of the law of the land, without express adoption, hence the federal courts had jurisdiction.[40] Congress should not specially provide for delivering over malefactors, nor aid in it, unless their offences lay outside the range of international law and yet be harmful to the foreign relations of the country. With these principles Jefferson also turned over to the committee a projected draft of a law to cover infractions of international law.[41]

The third great issue with Spain was the question of the navigation of the Mississippi. This was the mainspring in diplomatic relations with that country, carrying and urging along the other issues. It was not a new question when Jefferson undertook its settlement; there had been long negotiations on it while Jay was in Spain, and the policy of the United States had been settled for years. It was Jefferson's problem to gather all the arguments into a train, to bring Carmichael and Short into complete understanding and appreciation of this official viewpoint, and to induce, or force, Spain to accept as much as possible of it in a final agreement. Outlining his argument to Carmichael, he asserted that the United States had a right to the navigation both by nature and by treaty; that we could secure that right either by force, acting separately or in conjunction with Great Britain, or by negotiation. Spain should, for policy's sake, allow us more than the "naked" navigation; that is, grant a port near the mouth of the river. Moreover, in case of the neutrality of the United States, Great Britain could easily wrest the Floridas and Louisiana from Spain,—a disaster that could

---

[40] However, he doubted this proposition.
[41] Dec. 5, 1792, J. MSS.

be prevented by Spain's ceding the east bank to the United States and so acquiring the kind of a neighbor not given to conquest, one that would not cross the river for ages. For a string of barren, detached land, then, Spain could have an ally instead of an enemy.[42]

Washington had a strong opinion on the question. The policy of neutrality, adopted in 1793, has its preliminaries in his attitude from the beginning of his administration; but that policy faced toward American participation in the affairs of European balances, in Europe, rather than toward the quarrels or the ambitions of European powers developing in America and affecting the United States. His expressions in a letter to Lafayette are the best explanation of his views;

It seems to be our policy to keep in the situation in which nature has placed us, to observe a strict neutrality, and to furnish others with those good things of subsistance which they may want, and which our fertile land abundantly produces, if circumstances will permit us to do so. . . . Gradually recovering from the distresses in which the war left us, patiently advancing in our task of civil government, unentangled in the crooked politics of Europe, wanting scarcely anything but the full navigation of the Mississippi (which we must have, and as certainly shall have as we remain a nation), I have supposed, that, with the undeviating exercise of a just, steady and prudent national policy, we shall be the gainers, whether the powers of the old world may be in peace or in war, but more especially in the latter case. In that case our importance will certainly increase, and our friendship be courted. Our dispositions will not be indifferent to Britain or Spain. Why will not Spain be wise and liberal at once? [43]

Paris, rather than Madrid or Philadelphia, would have been Jefferson's choice for the scene of the negotiations with Spain. He advised Short to interest Lafayette and Montmorin in the cause, but the weakness of royalty and consequent distrust of the family compact, in the progress of the French Revolution, led him finally to favor Madrid.[44]   This communication reached Madrid by secret channels and the result was displayed in America when the chief Spanish *chargé*, Jaudenes, in a-

[42] "Heads of Consideration for Mr. Carmichael," Aug. 2, 1790, Writings, vol. vi, p. 123; letter enclosing it, ibid., vol. vi, p. 111.
[43] Washington to Lafayette, Aug. 11, 1790, Washington MSS. (Library of Congress).
[44] Jefferson to Short, Aug. 10, 1790, and Mar. 19, 1791, J. MSS.; Writings, vol. vi, p. 348.

conversation with Jefferson, told him that Spain was ready to treat at Madrid. The information was rushed to the President. Jefferson offered reasons why a response should be made at once, taking the opportunity to get his friend and former secretary, Short, made a commissioner to act with Carmichael. Although Jaudenes tried to back away from his verbal statement when he was asked to put it in writing, Jefferson held him to it, and a month later notified him officially of the new mission.[45]

March 7 and 18 Jefferson submitted two reports on the negotiations, covering completely the history of the points at issue, a long exposition of the American contentions, and his recommendations for the treaty.[46]   In the first report he assumed that the navigation of the Mississippi and recognition of the thirty-first parallel as the southern boundary were *sine qua non,* and devoted his attention to the commercial treaty for which Spain, it was hoped, was ready. Its basis should be that of the most favored nation, he argued, since Spain would not reciprocate on any other grounds. The French treaty rather than the Prussian should be the model, " because we have already supposed that Spain would never consent to those articles which give to each party access to all the dominions of the other." But among the articles which would need qualification was that which concerned asylum in our ports, for ships with prizes, as the stipulation in the latter part of the article "that no shelter or refuge shall be given in the ports of the one to such as shall have made prize on the subjects of the other of the parties," would forbid us in case of war between France and Spain, to give shelter in our ports, to prizes made by the latter on the former, while the first part of the articles would oblige us to shelter those made by the former on the latter; "a very dangerous covenant and which ought never to be repeated in any other instance." [47]

The senate having agreed to extending the negotiation to

---

[45] Jefferson to the Spanish Commissioners Jan. 21, 1792, J. MSS.; Writings, vol. vi, p. 377.
[46] Ibid., vol. vi, pp. 391, 414.
[47] Ibid., vol. vi, p. 398.

commerce, and having indicated a willingness to ratify a treaty constructed along the lines Jefferson had marked out,[48] he completed the second report and submitted it. It dealt with navigation of the Mississippi and the boundary. The history of the several exchanges of territory in the west, with the treaties defining them, was called on to support the contention that Spain had been cognizant of, and had agreed to, the limits claimed by the United States. No logic could prove that Spain had earned a right of possession above the line of 31°, by conquest or by occupation. Use of the river was a more debatable matter and required more extended argument. Was it a right or a privilege, which Spain could extend or withhold? The opinions of Vattel, Puffendorff, Wolff, and Grotius on such rights of navigation were quoted as favoring the American side; natural right was asserted; and, if stubborn pride left Spain a doubt, willingness to wage war was revealed.[49] Jefferson's accumulation of precedents, his acute understanding of international law, and his careful reasoning, made a case which the diplomats of the old world did not venture to answer.

The faint hope that these objects might be successfully negotiated was killed by three unfortunate and unpropitious factors. The first was that the papers containing the instructions were held up; another was Short's long delay at the Hague; and the third was the reconciliation between Spain and England, removing the former's urgency in settling her dispute with the United States.[50] Carmichael, too, was of no assistance. Jefferson's patience with him was almost at an end. "In truth it is so extraordinary a circumstance that a public agent, placed in a foreign court for the purpose of correspondence, should in three years have found means to get but one letter to us, that he must himself be sensible that if he could have sent us letters, he ought to be recalled

---

[48] Notes, March 16, 1792, J. MSS.

[49] "Extract from Report to the President," March 18, 1792, J. MSS.

[50] Short to Jefferson, Jan. 15, 1793, J. MSS.; Writings, vol. vii, p. 136.

as negligent, and if he could not, he ought to be recalled as useless. I have nevertheless procured his continuance in order to give him an opportunity which occurred of his rendering a sensible service to his country, and thereby drawing some degree of favor on his return." [51] The change in the Spanish attitude was to be seen both in Madrid and in Philadelphia. The negotiation was not to succeed while Jefferson was in office. Monroe's explanation was as correct as it was emphatic. " I have but little hope," he wrote Jefferson, " of a fortunate issue from the negotiation in Spain, for I observe that it is conducted on the part of that Court by Gardoqui a subtil and malignant little wretch, highly incensed against us for defeating him on that point here, and he well knows the support he recd upon that occasion from a party still high in office and all powerful in the present administration." [52] Jaudenes and Viar became more unreasonable, to such a point that all dealings with them were stopped and all points were referred to Madrid.[53] In a message to Congress on December 16, 1793, at the end of Jefferson's term as Secretary of State, and in language which Jefferson chose for him, Washington explained the status of the negotiations, showed the inter-position by Spain of non-essential details, " giving the appearance of a desire to urge on a disagreement," and expressed his hope for future establishment of more harmonious relations. But it was not an inspiring declaration. It was the acknowledgement of another treaty obstructed.[54] Yet Jefferson's plan was incorporated into a treaty within twenty-two months after his retirement, and the Pinckney Treaty bears his stamp in practically every article.

---

[51] Jefferson to Col. David, Mar. 22, 1793, J. MSS. This is not listed in the Calendar of Jefferson papers.

[52] Monroe, Writings, vol. i, p. 266. He referred, of course, to Jay.

[53] Writings, vol. vii, p. 443.

[54] Am. St. P., vol. i, p. 247. But see J. MSS., Dec. 16, 1793, for Jefferson's draft of this message.

CHAPTER VI

BRITISH AND FRENCH TREATIES

The lack of a sufficient treaty with Great Britain prevented the United States from having a true foundation for her foreign relations in the first ten years of her independence. Three-fourths of her trade was subject to the regulation of a foreign legislative body, and several trials at meeting that regulation with reciprocal discriminations met with failure. Only the favoring accident that the American nation became a strong commercial neutral in a critical war amended the unsatisfactory relationship.

If legal control of Anglo-American commerce was one-sided, all classes in England were content to believe that the economic advantages also rested with them. While Adams was in London he noted that no group, not even the opposition, favored a change. In fact, the English complaints on non-execution of the treaty of 1783, by the United States, bore the appearance of a defense against the American insistence that commercial relations be adjusted by a treaty; and so long as this emphasis could be maintained, no other reason was required for avoiding a commercial agreement. It was complete protection so long as Adams had no powerful friend at court,—as Lafayette was in France. There was, it is true, a committee of American merchants, formed to make protests, but their voice was drowned in the noise made by the whole body of British merchants. Through the spokesman of this latter body, Duncan Campbell, Jefferson and Adams made an attempt to open discussion with the ministry on the treaty of 1783, but without success.[1]

The deep enmity that Jefferson had toward the English government began in his experience as war governor in Virginia and remained with him while he was in Europe.[2] He

[1] Dip. Cor., vol. iii, p. 9.
[2] Jefferson to Francis Kinloch, Nov. 26, 1790, J. MSS.

preferred to divorce the tastes of his countrymen from the luxuries that he thought they indulged in by trading with England, but he realized that the advantages of longer credit would perpetuate that trade. While Americans were thus always in debt to British merchants it was difficult to remove the shackles from commerce, and so long as British regulations succeeded in holding American trade it seemed to Jefferson that independence was not realized. A letter to W. T. Franklin summed up his view: " They think their commerce indispensable to us. I think that if we are excluded from their W. Indies we shall be better without the commerce to Great Britain than with it. The luxuries of that country are familiar to us and will always tempt us to be in debt. They think we cannot unite to retaliate upon them. I hope we can, and that we shall exclude them from carrying our produce, if not suppress their commerce altogether. They think our whole people would be glad to return to their former dependence on them." [3]

The debts involved only two problems. One was interest during the war, and the other was prejudice in court action on recovery. His own debt to Alexander McCaul caused Jefferson to hold convictions on interest payments, the same, in fact, as he held at the time of instructing the envoys in Europe in the early part of 1784, that it was unallowable for the period of the war. But he was equally positive that the courts should be opened to British creditors. The judgments they obtained could be divided into equal annual instalments, the last due in 1790. " Since it is left for each nation to pursue their own measures in the execution of the late treaty, may not Congress with propriety recommend a mode of executing that article respecting the debts, and send it to each state to be passed into law. Whether England gives up the posts or not, these debts must be paid, or our character stained with infamy among all nations & to all times. As to the

---

[3] May 7, 1786; Jefferson to A. McCaul, April 19, 1786, J. MSS; Jefferson to Count von Hogendorp, Oct. 13, 1785, Writings, vol. iv, p. 466; Jefferson to Nathaniel Tracy, Aug. 17, 1785, in the Bixby Collection, (Ford).

satisfaction for slaves carried off, it is a bagatelle which if not made good before the last instalment becomes due, may be secured out of that." [4]

As Secretary of State, Jefferson began an investigation of the issues in our relations with Great Britain, exercising his customary thoroughness in collecting facts and, fortunately, putting his thoughts on them on paper. Whether or not the United States should pass a navigation act he reduced to the form of a brief, and bolstered his conclusions with figures from customs collectors' books. The United States, with large resources of raw materials would always find markets, and would take in exchange manufactured goods. Great Britain could not " subsist " Russia,[5] the only greater source of raw materials. He refuted Lord Sheffield's view that fishing vessels from the United States could take the West India trade during the winter months, by asserting that very few American-built vessels entered that trade, and that Great Britain could maintain ships in the West Indies more cheaply than the United States. After all, the competition between the two countries was in men, not in goods; at least one-third of the sailors on American vessels came over from Britain, between 1778 and 1790.[6]

This would intimate stricter rules on the part of the English, and, to meet their restrictions, equally effective restrictions should be adopted in Congress, in Jefferson's opinion. He arrived at the seat of government too late to influence the first Congress, although he favored and urged an act that would double the tonnage duties and eventually exclude vessels bringing goods not the produce of their own country, where our vessels were similarly excluded.[7] Coupled with this was his attitude on treaties, Great Britain being specially in mind, which should be for short terms, for

---

[4] Jefferson to Monroe, May 10, 1786, Writings, vol. v, p. 105.
[5] S. F. Bemis, Jay's Treaty, table opposite page 34.
[6] Notes, 1790, J. MSS. These pages have no other date.
[7] Jefferson to Edward Rutledge, July 4, 1790, Writings, vol. vi, p. 86.

7

the position of the United States was improving too rapidly to allow an unchangeable treaty just then.

The probability of an Anglo-American treaty was growing stronger in 1790. Gouverneur Morris had some results from his semi-insulting notes to the Duke of Leeds,[8] but far more decisive was the Nootka Sound crisis and the possibility of a rearrangement of the territorial balance in North America. Jefferson at last learned that the inclination to exchange ministers would bring an end to the secret agent and the conversations through Quebec. On August 12, 1790, he wrote Morris a letter in which he outlined the policy of the United States as it then stood, saying:

Besides, what they are saying to you, they are talking to us through Quebec; but so informally, that they may disavow it when they please. It would only oblige them to make the fortune of the poor Major, whom they would pretend to sacrifice. Through him, they talk of a minister, a treaty of commerce *and alliance*. If the object of the latter be honorable, it is useless; if dishonorable, inadmissable. These tamperings prove, they view a war as very possible; and some symptons indicate designs against the Spanish possessions adjoining us. The consequence of their acquiring all the country on our frontier, from the St. Croix to the St. Mary's are too obvious to you to need development, . . . a due balance on our borders is not less desirable to us, than a balance of power in Europe has always appeared to them. We wish to be neutral, and we will be so, *if they will execute the treaty fairly and attempt no conquests adjoining us.*[9]

This fear of an English conquest of Spanish North America was in Jefferson's mind when he answered the President's question relative to Lord Dorchester's anticipated march into Louisiana. There can be no doubt that Jefferson would have advised war against Great Britain if the Spanish and French had made motions toward a vigorous offensive alliance.[10] The permission, or refusal, to allow British troops to march through American territory was, therefore, merely incidental to the greater question.

---

[8] The Duke of Leeds to Morris, April 28, and Morris to the Duke of Leeds, April 30, 1790, British State Papers, Foreign Correspondence, vol. vi, Hammond Correspondence, (Henry Adams Transcripts, Library of Congress).

[9] Writings, vol. vi, p. 122.

[10] Notes, August, 1790, J. MSS. This reviews his entire reasoning. See also his letter to Franklin and Henry Laurens, March 31, 1790, asking for maps and information on the St. Croix boundary, J. MSS.

Gouverneur Morris found that his objects in London could be accomplished up to the point of explaining the American contention on the slaves and western posts only. He made the mistake of confiding to the French minister in London, de la Luzerne.[11] But a series of letters between Morris and the President, in which Morris's conduct was approved, elicited the same confirmation when reviewed by Jefferson. The two issues that he saw remaining for his own adjustment with an English minister in the United States, were the surrender of the posts and the recovery of the debts. For a treaty of commerce the United States was not willing to pay a price, certainly not the renunciation of France's friendship.[12] Within a few months after Morris had given up his mission, a committee of the Privy Council prepared a long report on the trade between the two countries in which appears an expression that was indicative of the official attitude.

The Committee are of opinion that negociation should first be tried before violent measures are taken. It has already been shown that the British government has taken no hostile step in consequence of the oppressive measures of many of the States, some allowance was to be made for the resentment natural after a war of seven years, and in this case, forbearance in every thing not essential, was a prudent as well as a dignified line of conduct. There was some reason to hope that time would diminish that hostile spirit, and recollection of former connections might lead the United States to a more favorable disposition towards G. Britain. Circumstances might also occur to detach them from their new connections and make the people of the two countries though no longer fellow subjects, friends at least, as before the war. Government has indeed been not altogether deceived—the new system is certainly more favorable to British navigation—and there can be no doubt from the proceedings of Congress, and from all that passed in their debates during the two last sessions, particularly in the American Senate, that a party is already formed in favor of a connection with Great Britain, which by moderation on her part may perhaps be so strengthened as to bring about in a friendly way, the objects in view.[13]

[11] Jared Sparks, Life of Gouverneur Morris, vol. i, p. 346; Washington's letter to Morris, Jan. 28, 1792, Washington, Writings, vol. xii, p. 98.

[12] "Report on letters from G. Morris to the President," Dec. 15, 1790, J. MSS. For Washington's message to Congress on this, see Am. St. P., For. Rel., vol. i, p. 121.

[13] " Report of a Committee of the Lords of the Privy Council on the Trade of Great Britain with the United States—January, 1791,"

While Jefferson advised Washington to hold aloof from mention of the posts, negroes, debts, and an exchange of ministers, he was urgently in favor of promoting legislation that would make a discrimination plain and strong enough to wound the British. On this he came into conflict with Hamilton. The two differed absolutely over the kind of message the President should send in to Congress, upon the failure of Morris to get any satisfactory response from the English ministry. Hamilton warned Jefferson against the danger of commercial warfare at a time when the United States needed revenue;[14] but the President's message followed Jefferson's advice and the report of the committee to which it was referred came back to the House in the form of a bill for regulation of trade. Not possible at this session of Congress, Jefferson thought it would be at the next, and, elated, sent copies to Short, Carmichael, and Humphreys for encouragement of France, Spain, and Portugal,—a veritable wall of restrictions against England.[15] Phineas Bond, English consul at Philadelphia, reported the bill to the Duke of Leeds as a measure to favor France, and as a cause of disagreement between the two secretaries.[16]

Sir John Temple, consul at New York, also reported Jefferson's hostility to the same statesman. " I am sorry to inform your Grace, that the Secretary of State's Party & Politics gains ground here, and I fear will have influence enough to cause Acts & Resolves which may be disagreeable to Great Britain, to be passed early in the next Session of Congress." [17] He said Beckwith's presence was disgusting to most Americans and a puzzle to himself. Washington wished Jefferson to

in J. MSS. This is in manuscript. It was probably furnished by W. T. Franklin. See Franklin to Jefferson, April 4, 1791, J. MSS.; also Bemis, p. 84.

[14] Hamilton to Jefferson, Jan. 11, 1791, Hamilton Works, vol. iv, p. 54.

[15] Jefferson to Short and Humphreys, March 15, and to Carmichael, March 17, 1791, J. MSS.

[16] Bond to the Duke of Leeds, March 14, 1791, Hammond Correspondence (Henry Adams Transcripts).

[17] Ibid., March 19, 1791.

ignore Beckwith and to make a statement to Lord Dorchester
on the supply of arms going out to the Indians from British
posts,—a practice so well proved that Jefferson need not make
a " delicate " communication about it.[18]   By the middle of
April, 1791, Jefferson knew of Beckwith's intimacy with
Hamilton and was therefore the less inclined to trust either
in later negotiations.[19]

The instructions given to George Hammond were based on
the principles contained in the report of the Privy Council's
committee, the preceding January. The retention of the posts
was due to American violation of the fourth and fifth articles
of the treaty of 1783; Great Britain would continue to allow
the United States unique privileges in ports of the kingdom,
but the West India trade would not be opened.   Discrimination in the United States should be stopped or retaliation
would be employed in England. If a commercial treaty should
be suggested, it would be agreeable to enter on it if the most
favored nation principle were first settled. If the United
States desired, maritime regulations might be inserted, except
to allow the United States to protect property belonging to
Great Britain's enemies in time of war,—" as it would be
more dangerous to concede this privilege to the Ships of the
United States than to those of any other Foreign Country." [20]

At the end of October, Hammond communicated to Jefferson his readiness to undertake the affairs of his mission. For
some weeks no definite answer was given.   Then he was asked
if he was empowered to deal with the withdrawal of the slaves
and the regulation of commerce.[21]   This was embarrassing.
He could give satisfaction on his instructions to deal with the
entire range of treaty infractions, but he had no such commission on commercial negotiations, and he learned that it

[18] Washington to Jefferson, April 4, 1791, Washington, Writings
(Ford) vol. xii, p. 31.
[19] Jefferson to Washington, April 17 and 24, 1791, Writings, vol.
vi, pp. 243, 247; to Monroe, April 17, 1791, ibid., vol. vi. p. 241.
[20] These instructions are in Hammond Correspondence (Henry
Adams Transcripts), July 4, 1791. This is a rough draft from Hawks-
bury to Leeds. For Grenville's modifications, see Bemis, pp. 89-94.
[21] Jefferson to Hammond, Nov. 29, 1791, J. MSS.

was Jefferson's hope to secure just this confession from him
so that in the report on commerce and fisheries, soon to be
laid before Congress, Jefferson could assert that Great Britain
had no intention of entering on a treaty.[22]   Hammond felt
obliged to commit himself in order to get any recognition at
all from Jefferson.

The first statement on infractions of the treaties, both preliminary and definitive, came from the American side.   It
concerned only two points, the negroes and the western posts,
with mere mention of the northeastern boundary.   It charged
British violation of the seventh article.   Although it was
accompanied with several documents to prove the culpability
of Sir Guy Carleton in deliberately violating the treaty, when
he refused to allow American Commissioners the right to
identify negroes on being taken aboard British ships, yet
when the mere " bagatelle " [23] view of the slaves is recalled,
no one can believe this argument was either pivotal or serious.
Even the more important indictment that the officers in
western posts were exercising jurisdiction over American
territory was clearly intended to draw Hammond out rather
than to express a final argument.[24]

While Hammond was composing his answer, the report on
commerce was delivered to Congress.   Since it arose from the
President's message of February 14, 1791,—instigated and,
in fact, dictated by Jefferson's anger over Morris's failure in
England,—it was expected to be a convincing proof of the
needs of retaliation upon Great Britain in general commercial
laws.   It did lead in that direction, but was not convincing.
After the worst had been said about the British navigation
acts, and methods of averting their bad effects recommended,
the report concluded: " When once it shall be perceived that
we are either in the System, or the Habit, of giving equal
advantages to those who extinguish our Commerce and Navi-

---

[22] Jefferson to Hammond, Dec. 5, 1791, ibid; Hammond to Grenville, Dec. 6, 1791, Hammond Correspondence (Henry Adams Transcripts).
[23] See above, p. 87.
[24] Jefferson to Hammond, Dec. 15, 1791, J. MSS.

gation by Duties and Prohibitions, as to those who treat both with liberality and justice, liberality and justice will be converted by all into Duties and Prohibitions." [25] A treaty had been proposed to Great Britain by the administration, but as the British were " already on as good a footing in law, and a better in Fact, than the most favored nation," they did not respond.[26]

The case of Thomas Pagan was referred by Hammond to Jefferson at this period.[27] It gave Jefferson an opportunity to demonstrate that the rule of law could fairly settle cases of dispute between citizens of two countries when their cases could not properly be considered objects of diplomacy. Pagan had captured an American vessel between the dates of preliminary and definite treaties, or on March 25, 1783, and carried his case for libel to Nova Scotia and then to the Lords of Appeal, where he was confirmed in rights of possession. But the owner in Massachusetts got judgment in the courts of that state, and on appeal to the state Supreme court was upheld. Pagan was put in jail. The appeal for interference went from Hammond to Jefferson and then to Edmund Randolph, by whose inquiry it was finally found that no appeal lay to the Supreme Court of the United States. The finality and the justice of the Massachusetts decision were defended in the letter by which Jefferson wound up the case: " However supposing the Court of Massachusetts to be the court of last resort in this case, it is then to be observed that the decision has been pronounced by the Judges of the land entrusted for their learning and integrity . . . that all the proceedings in the case have been marked with candor and attention towards Mr. Pagan, and that their decision can in no wise be charged with gross and palpable error." [28]

In the *Anas,* Jefferson revealed his discovery, early in 1792, that Hamilton was cutting the ground from under him, by-

[25] "Report on Commerce," J. MSS.
[26] Ibid.
[27] On this case see Jefferson to Hammond, Dec. 28, 1791, Jan. 28, 1792, and April 9 and 18, 1793, all J. MSS.
[28] Jefferson to Hammond, Sept. 13, 1793, J. MSS.

exchanging views with Hammond. "It was observable that whenever at any of our consultations anything was proposed as to Great Britain, Hamilton had constantly ready something which Mr. Hammond had communicated to him, which suited the subject, and proved the intimacy of their communications, insomuch that I believe he communicated to Hammond all our views and knew from him in return the views of the British court." [29]   Proofs of this, in Jefferson's opinion, could be found in Hamilton's attempt to induce the administration to enter on a tentative arrangement for a new commercial treaty with France, although the French minister, Ternant, had no powers for it, so that the same could be done with Hammond. Another case was Hamilton's objection to the report to Congress favoring retaliation against British shipping, on the ground that the delivery of the western posts would be jeopardized by it. The real motive, Jefferson came to believe, was to prepare the way for a new western boundary, arranged between Simcoe, Stevenson, Hammond, and Hamilton, to run by way of the Genesee and Alleghany rivers to the Ohio.[30]

The report to Congress was withheld while Hammond collected materials for his answer to Jefferson's allegations of the preceding December. Hammond had assistance from all angles, from Canada and the West, from his home government, from Hamilton, and especially from the British consuls. The Duke of Leeds sent a dispatch under date of January 5, 1792, containing information on a possible Spanish-American alliance, which Carmichael had written to Lord St. Helens, and a list of the debts owed by citizens of the United States to British subjects, prepared by the committee of North American merchants. Hammond delayed his communication so long that Washington lost patience and had Jefferson insist on its delivery. On March 5 it was

[29] March 11, 1792, J. MSS.
[30] Ibid., Bemis, p. 129; Hammond to Grenville, Jan. 9, 1792, Hammond Correspondence (Henry Adams Transcripts); "Extracts from Kirkland's letter" to Washington, Feb. 25, 1792, in J. MSS.

handed to Jefferson, with the explanation that it contained a complete statement.[31]

A beginning was made with the effect on Congress of Lord Carmarthen's answer to Adams in 1786. The circular letter sent to the governors of the States, advising that laws repugnant to the treaty be repealed, and that the courts be required to consider all cases without deviating from the true intent of the treaty, was proof that public faith had not been kept on the articles of the treaty. Some highly generalized statements were introduced charging that neither the United States nor the States had repealed laws in force prior to 1782; and that some legislation subsequent to the peace had been enacted, all contravening the treaty. The persons and estates of loyalists had been unjustly affected by state laws since the end of the war, and the recovery of debts seriously obstructed, although the treaty contained provisions to prevent these very things. Besides the debts, for which some figures were given,—there was, for example, not a single recovery of debt in the Southern States since the war,—Great Britain had to lose several million pounds in supporting her distressed subjects. On the contrary, American claimants regularly received judgments in English courts, even against loyalists.

On her part, Great Britain had merely suspended execution of the treaty. The United States had broken it first and were continually breaking it anew. As proof of this statement, as well as of the preceding charges, Hammond attached five appendices with some ninety-four cases of confiscation, banishments, illegal sale of property, and denial of justice on debts. Although the document was completed hurriedly, on account of the administration's anxiety to get negotiations to a point where the Indian wars could be quieted, by transfer of the forts, yet Hammond felt pleased with his accomplishment. "I flatter myself, my Lord," he wrote Grenville, "that this Statement will be found to be in exact conformity to the tenor of your Lordship's instructions, and to contain

[31] Am. St. P., For. Rel., vol. i, p. 193. Jefferson also had a letter press copy made to be kept in his papers.

a body of proof so complete and substantial as to preclude the probability of cavil and contradiction on the part of this government." [32]

Jefferson was unusually thorough in his preparations for the answer. He went through Hammond's citations of cases, finding all except thirteen of the ninety-four, and for these he requested the favor of an examination.[33] None was sent. Hammond explained that all except one were from the manuscript of "a friend," and he could only quote dates for the Rhode Island and Maryland acts. It was an admission that he could not verify his own statements. More than that, he observed to Grenville that the amounts in the table of debts sent him were exaggerated.[34] But an even greater discouragement to Hammond was the news he was obliged to give Jefferson, that Parliament was about to renew that part of the Navigation Acts, which prohibited importation of tobacco into England in foreign ships.[35] Jefferson tried to make this appear as a complete prohibition of the importation into England of American goods in American vessels, and had the President put this statement before Congress.[36] This forced Hammond to interpret the act; it applied only to smuggling of tobacco, he declared, and its scope was merely the islands of the channel.[37]

This disaster to a commercial *rapprochement* averted, or possibly from Jefferson's angle, the chance to break off negotions lost, the answer to Hammond was completed. The work done by Jay in 1786 in gathering reports from nearly all the States on their acts respecting the treaty and its purposes was brought up to date.[38] To these Jefferson added

[32] Hammond to Grenville, March 6, 1792, Hammond Correspondence (Henry Adams Transcripts).

[33] Jefferson to Hammond, March 30, 1792, J. MSS.

[34] Hammond to Grenville, April 5, 1792, Hammond Correspondence (Henry Adams Transcripts).

[35] 12 Car. 2, Ch. 18, sec. 3.

[36] Jefferson to the President, April 13, 1792, Writings, vol. vi, p. 477.

[37] Hammond to Grenville, April 14, 1792, Hammond Correspondence (Henry Adams Transcripts).

[38] Sec. Jour., vol. iv, p. 135. Copies of this correspondence are in the Jefferson papers for 1786-1788. For Hamilton's objections to the

the results of inquiries directed to the attorney-general of each State, to the senators and representatives of Georgia, Virginia, South Carolina, and Maryland, and to the chief clerk of the Supreme Court. With a careful examination of Hammond's cited cases, and of the text of the acts under which they had occurred, Jefferson was ready to meet Hammond's statement.

He refused to admit war legislation as debatable. Hence he removed all acts mentioned by Hammond belonging to the period previous to 1783, "as things out of the question." The acts relating to exile and confiscation he grouped together as had been done in the treaty, and disposed of them by showing that not a single act had been passed in any State on property except in arranging for property without title. As for Hammond's complaint on American envoys "recommending" what could not be effected, Jefferson showed that the word was purposely used instead of the usual "shall be done"; the practice of recommendation was so familiar to Americans that the envoys were neither ignorant nor deceitful in insisting on its use, with respect to the States, in the treaty. Recommendation had been made to the States in good faith, in fact, no less than thirty-four specific examples of compliance were brought forward as proof.

Before considering the question of debts, Jefferson examined the British infraction of the seventh article, requiring removal of armies, garrisons, and fleets without taking any negroes or other American property. Here he turned back upon the British Hammond's charge that the United States had first broken the treaty, by insisting that the British had never started to comply, and hence the Americans could not first have broken faith. Even as late as six months after the treaty, no orders had been given for removing the garrisons from forts located on soil admitted by the treaty to be within the boundaries of the United States. Weeks after the provisional stipulation against removing negroes was

communication to Hammond, see Hamilton to Jefferson, March, 1792, Hamilton, Writings, vol. iv, p. 60.

known to Sir Guy Carleton, they were being taken, and the infraction was admitted by the General. Because of these acts four States placed obstacles in the way of recovery of debts. But when Adams had intimations that the British court would meet the United States in adhering strictly to the treaty, Congress requested all of the States to discontinue all actions of any kind repugnant to the treaty, and, with the exception of one law in South Carolina, affecting natives equally with foreigners in recovering debts, all the States repealed their laws. Moreover, the federal courts were always open to cases arising under the treaty since treaties in the United States were federal law. Hammond's allegation that " in some of the Southern States, there does not exist a single instance of the recovery of British debt in their courts," was easily answered by reference to cases in which debts were collected. In concluding, Jefferson repeated, in elaborate form, his earlier conclusion that interest during the period of the war was not allowable.

This document overwhelmed Hammond. He admitted it to his home government as well as to Jefferson himself.[39] He had dinner with Jefferson and the two discussed their written arguments. Hammond was treated almost as a pupil. " The result was," Jefferson told Madison, " that he acknowledged explicitly that his court had hitherto heard one side of the question only, and that from prejudiced persons, that it was now for the first time discussed, that it was placed on entire new ground, his court having no idea of a charge of first infraction on them, and a justification on that ground of what had been done by our states, that this made it quite a new case to which no instructions he had could apply." [40]

Aside from another attack on commerce, and his correspondence with Pinckney, this is as far as Jefferson's direct influence on the British treaty extends. The ground was cleared and a treaty more probable than when he became Secretary of State, but his antagonism was too genuine and

[39] Hammond to Grenville, June 8, 1792, Hammond Correspondence (Henry Adams Transcripts).

[40] Jefferson to Madison, June 4, 1792, Writings, vol. vii, p. 100.

his methods too goading to give reason to suppose he could have concluded such a treaty. Within a few months after he had retired, Jay brought a negotiation to a conclusion and secured a treaty, of which Jefferson wrote Edward Rutledge: "I join with you in thinking the treaty an execrable thing . . . I trust the popular branch of our Legislature will disapprove of it, and thus rid us of this infamous act, which is really nothing more than a treaty of alliance between England and the Anglomen of this country, against the Legislature and people of the United States." [41]

The treaty of alliance with France presented no such clear issues. It was undertaken on the part of the United States with the single idea of gaining independence, and after the war had ended with that achievement, it had no further meaning. It is true that on some occasions Jefferson referred to it in half-hearted fashion when there was a possibility of promoting some interest of the United States. He discussed with Jay the question whether France considered herself bound to insist that Great Britain deliver the posts in the west, but feared to take it up with Vergennes because it would certainly lead to the question of how far we considered ourselves guarantors of their American possessions. [42] He reminded Vergennes, on one occasion, that France was bound by the alliance to guarantee the boundaries of the United States. Vergennes agreed, but remarked that they should be clearly established; and though Jefferson could assure him that England herself admitted them settled, the subject was filled with too many possibilities. "I feared, however, to press this any further, lest a reciprocal question should be put to me." [43]

Most common of all expressions used by Jefferson, and Adams as well, while in Europe, respecting the relation that the United States should bear to France's international problems was "neutrality." [44] Even Lafayette, contemplating a

[41] Jefferson to Edward Rutledge, Nov. 30, 1795, ibid., vol. viii, p. 199.
[42] Dip. Cor., vol. iii, p. 4.
[43] Ibid., p. 48.
[44] Jefferson to Carmichael, Dec. 15, 1787, Writings, vol. v, p. 363.

possible Anglo-French war, recommended it as the policy most useful to Americans and most favorable to France. " Every American harbor will offer a shelter for the French ships, a market for their prizes, and all the conveniences of repair and victualling; all which being consistent with treaties, gives no ground of complaint." [45]

The test of the alliance did not come, however, until 1793. Until that date, the treaty of commerce was being continually drawn into question,—a serious matter when there was no arrangement with England. The two countries, including the French West Indies, took virtually all of the exports of the United States, and could easily regulate our foreign trade out of existence. When the French *chargé,* Otto, complained of the tonnage acts of July 20, 1789, and July 20, 1790, as well as the acts of Massachusetts and New Hampshire, he insisted that they were in violation of the commercial treaty of 1778, which provided in its fifth article, against tonnage duties as well as for complete reciprocity in charges.[46] That better treatment was given in France than in the United States was the view held among the members of the National Assembly. They felt that the American trade was a losing venture for French merchants and a matter that required legislation similar to the English rules to put it on a profitable basis.[47]

Otto's letter was referred to Hamilton who advised a new treaty, certainly not ex parte concessions, for such preferences tended to stir up the hostility of those nations not favored.[48] Jefferson answered the complaint by showing the plain intention of the treaty, which was to grant fully reciprocal and most favored nation rights. If the French allowed American vessels exemption from the hundred sols duty on vessels coming from a foreign port, the United States were merely receiving a most favored nation right; in case of the tonnage duties, France was subjected to the same charges as the most

---

[45] Lafayette to Jay, Oct. 15, 1787, Dip. Cor., vol. i, p. 453.
[46] Otto to Jefferson, Dec. 13, 1790, J. MSS.
[47] Short to Jefferson, Oct. 21, 1790, J. MSS.
[48] Hamilton to Jefferson, Jan. 13, 1791, Hamilton, Writings, vol. iv, p. 54.

favored nation.[49]   But as his reply was to be laid before
Congress, he suggested that a trade of advantages be made,
exemption from tonnage duties in the United States for lessened duties on whale and fish oils in France.   This was
entirely unsatisfactory to Hamilton, for he saw one course
of revenue destroyed and no equivalent substituted, as well
as an unequal result with France greatly benefited.[50]   Jefferson, always hoping that the French commerce would replace the English, could defend his proposition only feebly.
" Tho' I am pointedly against admitting the French construction of the treaty, yet I think it essential to cook up
some favour which may ensure the continuance of the good
disposition they have towards us." [51]

The chief meaning of this argument was that the American opinion held the most favored nation principle was not
equivalent to free trade.   In fact, Jefferson's tendency was
less toward an untrammeled trade than it had been before
he returned to the United States. He conceived of this nation
as one hemmed in by foreign powers, forbidden to trade with
our neighbors and still subject to the European habit of
confounding force with right.   True, with some of the neighboring lands, the French West Indies, we were admitted to a
larger share of trade than ever before, and to the suspicions
of French merchants he felt it necessary to have Short reply
that the one principle most deeply rooted in the American
mind was that we should have nothing to do with conquest.
But in view of the extreme tax, almost a prohibition, laid on
the importation of tobacco in American vessels into France,
he continued in his letter:

" An exchange of surpluses and wants between neighboring
nations, is both a right and a duty under the moral law, and
measures against right should be mollified in their exercise." [52]   He hoped the National Assembly would correct the
decree and promote a treaty, " which shall melt the two

[49] Report to the President, Am. St. P., For. Rel., vol. i, p. 109.
[50] Hamilton to Jefferson, Jan. 11, 1791, Hamilton, MSS.
[51] Jefferson to Hamilton, Feb. 13, 1791, J. MSS.
[52] Jefferson to Short, July 28, 1791, Writings, vol. vi, p. 288.

nations as to commercial matters into one as nearly possible." [53]

When Ternant came as the new French minister, late in 1791, he had no instructions for a commercial treaty and indeed, did not expect any.[54] But Washington was anxious to avoid a repetition with France of the difficulty with England, and, against Jefferson's will, asked him to sketch out a form to answer the needs of the two countries as they then stood.[55] The form he proposed was based on the unusual grounds of native-citizen-rights, setting a maximum for advalorem duties and prohibiting premiums.[56] Short was instructed to continue overtures, but in advising him on this business as well as on the proper attitude he should hold toward the Revolution, it is open to question if Jefferson did not misrepresent Washington when he quoted him as saying for Short's benefit: " He added that he considered France as the sheet-anchor of this country and its friendship as a first object." [57]

This was at the beginning of the year 1793. Here the treaty of commerce was practically lost sight of in the more perplexing problem of neutrality, to which Jefferson gave undivided attention for the remainder of the year,—his last in the State Department. It is fitting, then, to consider the further development arising from the French treaties under that subject.

---

[53] Jefferson to Short, Aug. 29, 1791, J. MSS.
[54] Ibid., Nov. 24, 1791.
[55] See above, p. 52.
[56] Notes, Nov. 26, 1791, J. MSS.
[57] Jefferson to Short, Jan. 3, 1793, Writings, vol. vii, p. 202.

CHAPTER VII

Neutrality

Any mention of a war in Europe into which France might be drawn, invariably evoked from Jefferson an announcement that the true interests of the United States lay in a neutral position. Yet the opportunity to derive pecuniary advantages through the expansion of our commerce during a great war appealed to him as it did to most other Americans. He foresaw danger to the United States, too, if France were weakened, and even contemplated our becoming " sea-robbers under French colours." [1] Yet he was determined on ultimate neutrality. His opinions on European connections had settled into the conviction that our system should either exclude treaties entirely or make them exceptions, promoting our commerce but not entangling it with the politics of the old world.[2] This aloofness did not hold true in such degree where the West Indies were concerned. In August, 1789, Jefferson heard a rumor that the French government was about to relieve its financial distress by selling the French West Indies to Great Britain. While he put no confidence in the report, he carried the question to Montmorin. " He appeared unapprised of it, but to see at once that it would be a probable speculation between two parties circumstanced and principled as those two are. I apologized to him for the inquiries I had made in this business, by observing that it would be much against our interest, that any one power should monopolize all the West Indian Islands. ' *Pardi assurement,*' was his answer." [3]

The policy of neutrality was begun and continued by George Washington. Forced to hear himself called " gen-

[1] Jefferson to John Blair, Aug. 13; to Monroe, Aug. 5; to Alex. Donald, Sept. 17, 1787, J. MSS., to Jay, Oct. 8, 1787, Dip. Cor., vol. iii, p. 311.

[2] Jefferson to Dumas, Dec. 9, 1787, J. MSS.; to Edward Carrington, Dec. 21, 1787, Writings, vol. v, p. 375; to Col. Charles Lewis, Jan. 10, 1789, J. MSS.

[3] Dip. Cor., vol. iv, p. 137.

eral " a great part of his life, he was fundamentally a man of peace, and he inclined naturally toward neutrality because it was a peace policy. A letter to Lafayette in 1790 well expresses his clear vision of what line of action was best calculated to benefit the nation. " It seems to be our policy to keep in the situation in which nature has placed us, to observe a strict neutrality, and to furnish others with those good things of subsistence which they may want, and which our fertile land abundantly produces, if circumstances and events will permit us to do so." [4]

The furtherance and execution of the policy were distinctly Jefferson's. When Ternant came to the United States, he asked for advance payments on the debt, of at least three million livres, to furnish arms and supplies of food to the island of San Domingo. It was an opportunity not only to prove our gratitude for help of like nature during our Revolution, but also for a stroke of business, for the money would be paid out in the United States. But Hamilton raised objection to the legitimacy of the then French government, questioning its authority to give sufficient receipt. Jefferson then laid down the broad " principle of republicanism, to wit, that every people may establish what form of government they please, and change it as they please, the will of the nation being the only thing essential." [5]

The repetition of the request for advances on the debt for the unusual needs in France led Jefferson to indulge in " observations " which he nearly always committed to paper, and which are in his papers of January and February, 1793. He raised questions over the method of advancing payments, the propriety of risking cancellation on requisitions from the departments of the French executive, the probability of having the money, and such details, in all of which he was very much at sea.[6] Finance was not his forte and he ad-

---

[4] Aug. 11, 1790, Washington, MSS.
[5] Notes, Nov. 19, Dec. 27 and 30, 1792, J. MSS; Jefferson to the French Minister, Nov. 20, and to Morris, Dec. 30, 1792, ibid.
[6] January and February, 1793, J. MSS.; Writings, vol. vii, p. 216.

mitted it to Monroe.[7]   His impulse for delving into it at all
was the suspicion of Hamilton and the National Bank.

Information from France in the early part of 1793 indicated that the National Convention was opening the door to
a closer union with the American ally.   The obnoxious decree
on tobacco was repealed, the ports of all French colonies were
opened to Americans in particular, and arrangements made
to spend the money received on the debt in buying American
products.   This liberality was in spite of the wrath stirred up
by both Short and Morris, over whose demeanor and actions
LeBrun made strong complaint.[8]   Seeing plainly that Morris
could not remain at Paris, Washington suggested to Jefferson
that he return to his former post, if he still intended to resign
from the cabinet.   But the prospect of crossing the Atlantic
again was more than Jefferson would consider.   Why, he
asked, should not Morris and Pinckney exchange places?
For which the President had the ready answer that if Morris
were offensive in Paris, he could hardly be stationed so near,
and in so important a post, as London.[9]

A more potent factor in holding Jefferson both in America
and in the cabinet was that he foresaw in Genêt's coming a
shifting of the scene of action to Philadelphia.   The whole
administration realized that France could not long avoid
war.   War meant that the speculations of American states-
men during the ten years of independence must at last
become working principles.   The change in the French government, now a republic, was accompanied by a change in
ministers to the United States, the monarchist Ternant being
replaced by the extreme republican Genêt, and the knowledge
that the latter was on his way precipitated a lively cabinet
discussion over the effects of the alliance.

A series of twenty-nine questions on the treaties was pro-
pounded by Hamilton and Jefferson at the end of February,
1793.   They do not seem to have been answered until the two

---

[7] Jefferson to Monroe, Jan. 14, 1793, Writings, vol. vii, p. 207.
[8] Jefferson to the President, Jan. 13, 1793, J. MSS.   This includes
letters between Morris and LeBrun, Foreign Minister, which Jefferson translated for Washington.
[9] Notes, February 20, 1793, J. MSS.

gave in their long written opinions on the question of repudiating the whole obligation of the treaties, about two months
later. But the questions forecast in almost prophetic manner
the later neutrality problems,—the rights of using American
ports, outfitting originally and of supplementing, adding to
crews and giving commissions to citizens of the United
States, exclusion of all other than French privateers, bringing, keeping, and selling prizes in our ports, establishing
prize courts,—in a word, the probable cases arising under
article eleven of the treaty of alliance, and seventeen and
twenty-two of the treaty of commerce.[10]

Jefferson continued to hope that Great Britain would fear
the aid the United States might give to France, and so would
be forced to come to a quick decision on a commercial treaty.
British restraint on American vessels carrying provisions to
France he believed would be a sufficient cause for war, and
his hope of influencing Congress more than Washington made
him trust that a special session would be called.[11] Hammond
had been warned of the dangers in Genêt's mission and instructed to counteract his efforts to equip privateers, and to
endeavor to hold the United States to an impartial conduct.[12]
Hammond believed the United States was bound by the
treaties, but judged that Great Britain could stop her participation in the war by blockading her coast.[13]

But the thought of giving aid to France was not a practical proposition, for further advances on the loans were
refused to Ternant, and even while Genêt was in the South,
Washington submitted to Jefferson a request to consider the
best means of preparing for " a strict neutrality." Thus
neutrality became the policy of the administration, and the
only problem was how best to put it into effect.[14] When
Washington returned to Philadelphia, he called a meeting of

[10] J. MSS., February (1793). No date of the month is given. The
year is not on the original and has been erroneously supplied as
"1791."
[11] Jefferson to Madison, March, 1793, Writings, vol. vii, p. 250.
[12] Grenville to Hammond, March 12, 1793, Hammond Correspondence (Henry Adams Transcripts).
[13] Hammond to Grenville, March 7, 1793, ibid.
[14] "Substance of Answer," April 18, 1793, J. MSS.

the cabinet to decide on receiving Genêt and on the validity of the treaties.[15] The members were divided, Hamilton and Knox against Jefferson and Randolph. Their differences were so decided that time was allowed for the preparation of written opinions; but meanwhile Washington laid before them a list of thirteen questions on a proclamation and on our conduct respecting the guarantee of the French islands.[16] The first contained the proposition for a proclamation of neutrality, questioning the use of that word; the second, the reception of Genêt. Both were decided affirmatively.[17] The remaining questions, being less pressing, were left to the written opinions to answer.

The proclamation was drafted by Randolph. Had Hamilton been successful in impressing his opinions on the President, he would have presented a form drawn up by Jay, about two weeks earlier. This copy is in the Hamilton manuscripts, with a letter from Jay, saying: " Your Letters of the 9th inst. were this Day delivered to me, as I was preparing to go out of town—The subject of them is important—I have not Time to judge decidedly on some of the points—the enclosed will show what my present Ideas of a proclamation are—it is hastily drawn—it says nothing of Treaties—it speaks of neutrality, but avoids the Expression because in this country often associated with others." [18]

But the ideas were those of Jefferson and the two other Virginians in the administration, Washington and Randolph. The document was issued on April 22. Two days before, Jefferson notified Pinckney of the course he was to pursue, in words very similar to the proclamation itself. " You may on every occasion give assurances which cannot go beyond the real desires of this country to preserve a fair neutrality in the present war, on condition that the rights of neutral nations are respected in us, as they have been settled in.

---

[15] Washington to Jefferson, April 12, 1793, Washington, Writings, vol. xii, p. 278.
[16] Jefferson believed these were framed by Hamilton (Notes, April 18, 1793, J. MSS.)
[17] Washington, Writings, vol. xii, 280.
[18] Hamilton MSS., April 11, 1793.

modern times." [19]   Yet the United States had not been officially notified of the war when the proclamation was issued, and moreover, by its own words, it was addressed as a warning to American citizens, not as a notification to foreign governments.[20]   It was, however, communicated to the foreign ministers residing in the United States as well as to the belligerent governments through the respective American ministers at those courts.   A copy was also sent to the governor of each State.[21]

This policy met with general approval.   True, Rufus King probably expressed the opinion of a considerable group in saying that he " could have wished to have seen in some part of it the word ' Neutrality,' which every one would have understood and felt the force of ";[22] but even Hammond found that " this paper, though worded with considerable caution, appears to admit but of little cavil, and to be as explicit in its import as could have been expected from a government of which the Executive branch is so constituted as its that of the United States." [23]

The delayed answer to Washington's thirteen questions was made on April 28, six days after the proclamation.   The first and second were already answered, although the second— Genêt's reception—was not yet acted on; and the seventh to tenth, inclusive, concerning the guarantee, were left to be considered if future circumstances made it necessary.   The remaining questions, answered in the opinion, were:

Quest. III.   If (Genêt be) received shall it be absolutely or with qualifications;—and if with qualifications, of what kind?
Quest. IV.   Are the United States obliged by good faith to consider the Treaties heretofore made with France as applying to the present situation of the parties—May they either renounce them, or hold them suspended 'till the Government of France shall be established?

---

[19] April 20th, 1793, J. MSS.
[20] Jefferson to Ternant, Van Berckel, and Hammond, April 23, 1793, J. MSS.
[21] Ibid.   Also Jefferson to Morris, Pinckney, and Short, April 26, 1793; and to "All the Governors except of Penna.," April 26, 1793, J. MSS.
[22] King to Hamilton, April 24, 1793, Hamilton, MSS.
[23] Hammond to Grenville, May 17, 1793, Hammond Correspondence (Henry Adams Transcripts).

Quest. V. If they have the right is it expedient to do either, and which?

Quest. VI. If they have an option, would it be a breach of Neutrality to consider the Treaties still in operation? [24]

Jefferson began his answer by refuting the position Hamilton took in the cabinet meeting on April 19.[25] This was that to continue the treaties with a new French government was equivalent to making them anew, and, since the clause of guarantee would be included, to make a treaty with a guarantee while war was going on would be a breach of neutrality. Hence the treaties should be renounced. Jefferson admitted the ingenuity of this argument without subscribing to its soundness, and conformed his opinion to the line Hamilton had marked out. The change in the form of government in France, instead of being a cause for ending the treaties, made no difference in their obligation or their force. The treaties bound the states, not their governments. Hamilton alluded to the clause of guarantee as so dangerous to the United States that it ought to be renounced, leaving it to France to say whether the remainder of the treaty was binding. On this Vattel was quoted to the effect that an alliance which became useless, dangerous, or disagreeable might be repudiated. But Jefferson gathered together the authority of Grotius, Puffendorff, Wolf, and Vattel to show that a consensus of opinion was against this idea; in truth an extended search of Vattel's own writings contradicted the one excerpt. Thus the danger of the alliance was not proved even as to the guarantee. It was " neither extreme, nor iminent, nor even probable."

Moreover, the moral obligation was too great to break down under the weight of a " possible " danger. Jefferson subscribed to the social contract theory, whereby the moral obligations of nations were analogous to the duties an individual was bound to by his conscience. To make contracts void by the possibility of danger would mean that there never would be contracts. But if the danger lay in the opening of our ports to French privateers and their prizes, the Dutch and

---

[24] See above, p. 107.   [25] Writings, vol. vii, p. 283.

Prussians had subscribed to it in treaties with us, and the treaty between England and France contained an exactly similar article, putting us in her harbors " on the same footing on which she is in ours, in case of a war of either of us with France." His conclusion was that " the not renouncing the treaties now is so far from being a breach of neutrality, that the doing it would be the breach, by giving just cause of war to France." [26]

But however much Jefferson delighted in overthrowing

---

[26] Ibid. Hamilton's opinion is in his Works, vol. iv, p. 369. There are three entries in the Jefferson papers, two under date of September 30, 1787, and one of April, 1793, purporting to be instructions given to Moustier, decidedly contrary to the spirit of an ally. One of those dated 1787 is in French, the other a translation in Jefferson's handwriting. Genêt handed the French version to Jefferson as an indictment of the old regime. The one now placed in the papers as of April, 1793, (the dating is questioned) follows:

" Proofs of the Machiavelism of the Cabinet of Versailles. Extract of a letter of M. de Vergennes to the *Chargé d'affaires* of France with the U. S.

'Versailles, July 21, 1783.
' The future existence of the Congress presents important questions to discuss, and I foresee that it will be some time before they will be decided. I think as you do that the preservation of the Congress would suit us; but what perhaps suits us better is that the U. S. should not acquire the political consistence of which they are susceptible—because everything convinces me that their views & their affections will be very versatile, & that we cannot count on them, if ever there happen to us new discussions with England.'

This opinion has been entirely adopted since, & has served as the basis of the instructions given in 1787 to M. de Moustier."

The others, of September 30, 1787, were letter-press copies. The translated copy runs:

" Extract from the Instructions given to the Cte. de Moustier Sep. 30, 1787.

' The Ct de Moustier will have seen in the correspondence of the Sr Otto that the Americans are occupied with a new constitution. This object interests but weakly the politics of the King. his Majesty thinks, on the one hand, that these deliberations will not succeed on account of the diversity of affections, of principles, & of interests of the different provinces, on the other hand, that it suits France that the U. S. should remain in their present state, because if they should acquire the consistence of which they are susceptible, they would soon acquire a force or a power which they would be very ready to abuse. Notwithstanding this last reflexion, the Minister of the king will take care to observe a conduct the most passive, neither to shew himself for, nor against the new arrangements on which they are occupied, and when he shall be forced to speak, he will only express the wishes of the king, & his own personal wishes, for the prosperity of the U. S."

Hamilton in an argument over legal points, his application
of the rule of neutrality during the remainder of 1793 was
not consistent with the spirit and intention of the treaties. It
may be allowed that the treaty of alliance had one particular
object, namely, American independence, but when it is taken
with the seventeenth and twenty-second articles of the commercial treaty, it has no meaning at all unless it means that
French warships were to be directly aided in their operations.
Certainly if John Paul Jones had not been allowed to outfit
privateers in French ports and to operate from them against
the English, in the Revolutionary War; if France had depended on very strict construction of the treaty clauses as
reasons for not lending aid, or even direct encouragement,
in that war, an alliance would have been useless, the very
word a mockery. Neutrality and alliance are mutually exclusive, in action.[27]

But "Mr. Genêst" had no sooner arrived in Charleston
than the problem of executing the order of neutrality began.[28]
The privateers he commissioned forced the question with the
administration. Randolph gave his opinion for expelling
them from American harbors. The practice, he judged, was
an attack on sovereignty. The remedy was to put all such
illegally commissioned vessels out of the protection of the
United States. But foreign-built vessels owned by Americans
were entitled to passports, because they were as much neutral
property as home-built vessels.[29]

Besides the vessels carried into Charleston harbor by privateers, the French warship *l'Embuscade* began to operate in
the very vicinity of the American government. The most
important of her early captures was the British ship *Grange,*
taken in Delaware Bay—in territorial waters—and carried as
a prize to Philadelphia. Hammond made a vigorous protest
to Jefferson. It was communicated to the French minister

---

[27] See Citizen Adet to Timothy Pickering, Nov. 15, 1796, Duane's
Pamphlets, vol. lix, p. 29 (Library of Congress).
[28] Jefferson to T. M. Randolph, April 21, 1793, J. MSS. This is
not listed in the Calendar.
[29] "Minutes of reasons which operated with E. R. in advising
the expulsion of the Genêt privateers," May, 1793, J. MSS.

and he was asked to detain the prize until the facts were officially established and the decision of the government made.[30] Hamilton drew Randolph to his side on this case and the two demanded of Washington that this insult be met with action instead of the excuse that Jefferson would allow,—that the captures up to date should be overlooked because orders to prevent them had not been given throughout the country.[31] Randolph gave Washington the information that most of the merchants of the country favored restitution of the prizes,[32] but when it was brought before the cabinet he took the position that nothing more than ordering the privateers away could be done. At this meeting, May 20, Jefferson argued that nothing at all could be done as to prizes already made, for the fair inference from article twenty-two of the treaty was that if the enemies of France could not fit out privateers, the implication was that France could. If they had come in on that understanding, surely they had committed no violation. The United States had not forbidden them, although they could do so for the future. But he was overruled. Washington adopted Randolph's opinion that the privateers should be ordered away and nothing said of previous captures.[33]

Jefferson accepted this decision as a victory of the " Anglomen," and it stirred his feelings against Great Britain to the point of intense bitterness.[34] Nevertheless his friendliness toward Genêt gradually cooled, and he became the active agent of the administration in deciding the difficult cases in the application of its policy. He believed that the United

---

[30] Randolph to Jefferson, May 2; Jefferson to Tench Coxe, May 3, 1793, J. MSS.; Jefferson to the Minister Plenipotentiary of France, May 3, 1793, Writings, vol. vii, p. 307; to the Minister of Great Britain, May 3, 1793, ibid., p. 306.

[31] Washington to Hamilton, May 7, 1793, Washington, Writings, vol. xii, p. 289; Hammond to Jefferson, May 8, 1793, J. MSS.; Hamilton's opinion, May 15, and Jefferson's, May 16, 1793, Washington, MSS.; Hamilton to Washington, May 15, Hamilton, Writings, vol. iv, p. 408.

[32] Randolph to the President, " private," May 18, 1793, Washington, MSS.

[33] Notes, May 20, 1793, J. MSS.

[34] Jefferson to W. V. Murray, May 21, 1793, J. MSS. In this letter he speaks of England as the " *hostis humani generis.*"

States district attorneys and the federal courts should handle
the infractions that occurred in the various ports, whereas
Hamilton regarded the collectors of the ports, acting under
orders from the Treasury Department, as the proper persons
to assume that authority in first instances.[35] To make sure
that the orders of the government would be effective, General
Knox was asked to advise the governors of the States to call
out the militia in aid of the civil authorities, when necessary,
and to detain the " attackers " of neutrality until their cases
could be laid before the President for decision.[36]

When Genêt arrived in Philadelphia he agreed to restore
the *Grange,* in a spirit of sacrificing a right. As Jefferson
appeared inclined to offer him advice and an impersonal kind
of friendship, he opened a remarkable correspondence with
letter-orations couched in grandiloquent language and super-
fervid phrases, conveying the greatness of his government's
generosity to the American ally and the hope of cementing
their fraternal relations.[37] He defended his encouragement
of privateers at Charleston on the grounds of the treaties, his
instructions, and the approval of Governor Moultrie of South
Carolina. The use of his letters of marque and the enrolling
of American citizens in the crews of the privateers were defended in the same way.[38] He had a counter-complaint to
urge in his objection to the punishment of Gideon Henfield,
an American who had entered the service of France and was
in jail awaiting trial for his violation of neutrality. Randolph answered by noting that no foreign government, or its
minister, had any place in the determination of the crimes

[35] Jefferson to the Governor of Virginia, May 21, 1793; " E. R.
to Th. J.," May 9, 1793; Washington to the Heads of Departments,
July 29, 1793, J. MSS.

[36] " Sketch of a letter," May 21, 1793, J. MSS.

[37] In defense of Genêt it may be said that at first, aside from his
style of writing, he was literally following instructions. His letters
are in the American State Papers, Foreign Relations, vol. 1, in Jefferson's papers, in the Annual Reports of the American Historical
Association (F. J. Turner,—these in French), and a few are in
Correspondence between Genêt and Officers of the Federal Government (printed), Library of Congress.

[38] Am. St. P., vol. i, p. 150.

of citizens of the United States; that Henfield had broken the neutrality ruling and hence was punishable.[39]

During June and July, Genêt and Hammond made Jefferson's office a busy one. A final decision that the early prizes would not be restored, except for the *Grange,* was given after Hammond's insistence. He was told that as the commissions under which the privateers sailed could not have been invalidated by the United States, the property could not be recovered except through the courts.[40] Although he presented every case of unneutral character that came to his attention, Hammond found the general course of the government to be satisfactory. He summed it up in a report to Grenville as fear of the pro-French party and a genuine desire to restrain their own citizens.[41]

On the other hand, Genêt was exasperated over his failure to break down the administration's determination to enforce neutrality. On June 8, he introduced in a letter to Jefferson a rather defiant note:

" I have instructed the consuls not to grant letters but to the captains, who shall obligate themselves, under oath and security, to respect the territory of the United States, and the political opinions of the President. . . . This is all that the American government can expect from our deference." [42]

Less than a week later, June 14, he practically demanded that Washington order Hamilton to adjust with him " immediately " the payments on the debt.[43] On the same occasion he wrote of the " contempt " of the United States for the treaties, when the sale of prizes *William* and *Active* was stopped, and the intended privateer *Catherine* was seized and detained in New York harbor by Governor Clinton.[44] A

---

[39] It is to be noted that this rule was not yet *law.* On Henfield's case, see Wharton, State Trials, p. 66.

[40] Jefferson to the Minister Plenipotentiary of Great Britain, June 3, 1793, J. MSS.

[41] Hammond to Grenville, June 10, 1793, Hammond Correspondence (Henry Adams Transcripts). Jefferson to the Minister Plenipotentiary of Great Britain, June 3, 1793, J. MSS.; C. de Witt, Jefferson and American Democracy, appendix VII.

[42] Am. St. P., For. Rel., vol. i, p. 151.

[43] Ibid., p. 157.

[44] " Protest of Citizen Hauterive," June 24, 1793, J. MSS.

335]NEUTRALITY

further grievance against the same governor, reported by Citizen Hauterive, was his decision to enforce the twenty-four hour rule against the warship *l'Embuscade,* in favor of the English packet. Genêt insisted that it was not a general rule, certainly never observed by England. On June 17, he issued a notice to the people of the United States instructing them as to the means of payment for provisions destined for the West Indies, and appealing for aid to their " brethren " in France.[45]

The consequence of these rash statements were disastrous to the party upon which Jefferson depended. Without much regard for the personal fate of Genêt, Jefferson feared the effect on the " republicans " in the United States. He confided to Monroe: " I am doing everything in my power to moderate the impetuosity of his movements, and to destroy the dangerous opinion which has been excited in him, that the people of the U. S. will disavow the acts of their government, and that he has an appeal from the Executive to Congress, and from both to the people." [46]

Jefferson's adherence to the proclamation had never been from the heart. It was not only a " milk and water " pronouncement; it was, in his opinion, an executive usurpation and beyond the constitutional powers of the President.[47] Monroe agreed in this, at least in that part of it which would intimate that it was a legislative rather than an executive function. The Legislature was given the positive right to declare war, hence by inference it had the negative power to maintain " no war," or neutrality.[48] The question of the propriety of the proclamation was being reopened, at the end of July, by articles in the " Gazette of the United States," written by Hamilton under the pen name of " Publius." His arguments were those he had opposed to Jefferson's in cabinet meetings in April and May. Jefferson was eager to.

---

[45] " Genêt to the Citizens of the U. S.,"—a copy (June 17, 1793, J. MSS.).
[46] June 28, 1793, Writings, vol. vii, p. 415.
[47] Jefferson to Madison, June 29, 1793, Writings, vol. vii, p. 418; C. G. Fenwick, Neutrality Laws of the United States, p. 22.
[48] Monroe to Jefferson, Monroe Writings, vol. i, p. 261.

have them combatted. He first suggested to Madison that he should answer these "heresies," then finally forced the matter on him.[49]

This partisan conflict had no effect on the execution of the policy. It was too far advanced to be abandoned, or even materially altered. But the fact that no strictly legal support had been given to it was cause for an appeal by the cabinet to the justices of the Supreme Court for an opinion on a series of questions covering the obligations of the United States in the treaties and under international law, as both had been involved in the experience of the administration from the date of the proclamation. They were outlined by Hamilton, but Jefferson added a few to the list, all of the same nature as those of the Secretary of the Treasury.[50] The court properly refused to give opinions on these matters of policy and international law.

The outstanding case of breach of neutrality was that of the *Little Sarah*. This vessel was an English prize, brought in to Philadelphia and there refitted. Genêt did not deny that her armament was enlarged, nor that Americans were added to her crew, when Jefferson asked him for the facts.[51] The suspicion that she was about to sail led Governor Mifflin to inquire if that were Genêt's intention. His secretary, Dallas, having called on Genêt at midnight on Saturday, July 6, without getting any satisfaction, Jefferson had an interview with Genêt the next day. Genêt was much excited and would not talk seriously until he had become calmer, when Jefferson gave him some strong advice on the threat of appealing to Congress, and asked him for an assurance that the vessel would not sail before the President's return. Genêt did not make such a promise, equivocating and insist-

---

[49] Jefferson to Madison, June 29, July 7, Aug. 3 and 11, 1793, Writings, vol. vii, pp. 418, 436, 463, 471.

[50] Hamilton, Works, vol. iv, p. 193. Lodge says Hamilton objected to placing these questions before the members of the court, but that Washington yielded to Jefferson's insistence (ibid., footnote, p. 197). But see also Jefferson, Writings, vol. vii, p. 452, and footnote.

[51] Genêt to Jefferson, July 9, 1794, Am. St. P., For. Rel., vol. i, p. 163; M. Woodbury, Public Opinion in Philadelphia, 1789-1801, p. 79.

ing that she would not be ready to sail for some time.[52]
Going into a cabinet meeting of only Hamilton, Knox, and
himself, he met and combatted their opinion that a battery
should be erected on Mud Island to prevent the vessel from
passing down the river. He put it on the grounds of his
supposed agreement with Genêt, in part, but much more on
his unwillingness to give cause for war over two cannon, and
to allow the monarchies of the world to see the only existing
republics fighting each other.[53]

Washington was not at all pleased with this reasoning.
His command to Jefferson was equivalent to a reprimand.
" What is to be done," he wrote, " in the case of the *Little
Sarah,* now at Chester?—Is the Minister of the French
Republic to set the acts of this government at defiance *with
impunity?* and then threaten the Executive with an appeal to
the people.—What must the World think of such conduct and
of the government of the United States in submitting to
it? " [54] Jefferson's course seems hardly sincere. On July 7,
he wrote Madison a severe indictment of Genêt. " Never in
my opinion, was so calamitous an appointment made, as that
of the present Minister of F. here. Hot headed, all imagina-
tion, no judgment, passionate, disrespectful & even indecent
towards the P. in his written as well as verbal communications, talking of appeals from him to Congress, from them
to the people, urging the most unreasonable & groundless
propositions, & in the most dictatorial style, &c, &c., &c." [55]
Yet three days later, in his notes, he could write, concerning
the Sunday interview: " . . . he did in some part of his
declamation to me drop the idea of publishing a narrative or
statement of transactions but he did not on that nor ever did
on any other occasion in my presence, use disrespectful expressions of the President." [56]

---

[52] Notes, July 10, 1793, J. MSS.
[53] Opinion, Writings, vol. vii, p. 437; Jefferson to the President,
July 11, 1793, ibid., vol. vii, p. 438.
[54] Washington to Jefferson, July 11, 1793, Washington, Writings,
vol. xii, p. 302.
[55] Jefferson to Madison, July 7, 1793, Writings, vol. vii, p. 436.
[56] Notes, July 10, 1794, J. MSS. Dallas was positive that Genêt

This experience,—the *Little Sarah* as *Le Petit Democrat* having defied the order and escaped,—determined Washington to ask for Genêt's recall. Jefferson foresaw the rupture, admitting that "there has been something to blame on both sides, but much more on his." [57] The President mentioned in a cabinet meeting, on July 23, his own opinion that Genêt's conduct should be brought to the attention of his government by Gouverneur Morris and his recall asked for, "and in the meantime that we should desire him either to withdraw or cease his functions." [58] Hamilton urged the President to strong action, proposing to lay the whole business before the public in order to prevent the overthrow of the government by a faction. Jefferson was required to bring all the correspondence to and from the French minister, to a meeting at which Randolph would be able to be present; but since the Attorney-General was "engaged at the Supreme Court" longer than was expected, Washington asked that the letters be brought to his house, where the cabinet was invited to dinner. [59]

At this and succeeding meetings the decision was made. Jefferson reported it to Madison:

"We have decided unanimously to *require the recall of Genêt. He will sink the republican* interest if they do not *abandon him. Hamilton presses eagerly an appeal, i. e.,* to the *people.* Its consequences you will readily seize, but *I hope we shall prevent it* tho' the Pr. *is inclined* to it." [60]

Randolph feared Jefferson would base the recall on subleties and incidentals, which was possible, and to prevent such a possibility he wrote a list of charges as he had been asked to do, noting five specific points on which Genêt was guilty. [61] They included his granting commissions to privateers after agreeing to desist; his having consuls continue

had used the expression "appeal from the President to the People" (Hamilton to Rufus King, August 13, 1793, Hamilton MSS.).
[57] Jefferson to Madison, July 14, 1793, J. MSS.
[58] Notes of a cabinet meeting, July 23, 1793, ibid.
[59] Washington to Jefferson, July 31, 1793, Washington, Writings, vol. xii, p. 313.
[60] Jefferson to Madison, Aug. 3, 1793, Writings, VII, 463.
[61] Randolph to Jefferson, August 4, 1793, J. MSS.

their exercises of admiralty functions, after promises to the contrary; his sending out *Le Petit Democrat* against the wishes of the government; his reprehensible language concerning the President; and his attempts to interfere with the prosecutions of Americans who had enlisted on French privateers. After some differences of opinion between Hamilton and Jefferson over the phrasing of the letter to Morris, asking for the recall, it was sent on August 16. It was a lengthy review of the entire career of Genêt in the United States, and, with Jefferson's notes on the cabinet-meetings, affords the best apology for his conduct of the State Department and, in fact, for the American government's position during the critical days of 1793.[62]

Washington also favored the execution of neutrality by the collectors of customs. When this came up again,[63] Jefferson once more offered to resign, for it was a considerable victory for Hamilton, and Jefferson felt that it proved a lack of confidence to remove the administration of the ordinance from his department, where he was convinced it belonged.[64] But Hamilton did not differ materially from Jefferson's views, in a " Circular " to the collectors. The eight rules it contained scrupulously observed the treaties and made " unlawful " only the original outfitting of vessels for war use, and the enlistment of American citizens in service of a belligerent.[65] Along with this, was the decision to demand the restitution of all prizes made subsequent to June 5 by privateers fitted out in American harbors.[66]

The continued influx of complaints over the actions of British and French vessels was not abated during the autumn and fall of 1793, although precedents had been accumulated on most of the infractions. Jefferson postponed his resignation from September 30 to the end of the year, but decided

[62] Writings, vol. vii, p. 475. Hammond thought war would follow if France refused to make the recall (Hammond to Grenville, August 10, 1793, Hammond Correspondence, Henry Adams Transcripts).
[63] See above, page 113.
[64] Notes, Aug. 6 and 11, 1793, J. MSS.; Monroe to Jefferson, Sept. 3, 1793, Monroe, Writings, vol. i, p. 273.
[65] Am. St. P., For. Rel., vol. i, p. 45.
[66] Cabinet on Restitution of Prizes, Aug. 3, 1793, J. MSS.

to visit Monticello from the first of October to the middle of November,—a season when Washington was due to be absent also. A scourge of yellow fever afflicted Philadelphia at the end of the summer and he moved out to Germantown, although he went into the city to his office each day. His most flagrant case in this period was from Boston. A French privateer sent a prize into the port and it was placed under arrest by the United States marshal. M. du Plaine, French consul, collected an armed force from one of his vessels in the harbor and rescued the prize by force.[67] Jefferson asked Washington to revoke the consul's exequatur and followed it up by a " Circular to the French Consuls," marking out decisively the limits of their jurisdiction.[68]

Genêt had been in New York endeavoring to prepare a fleet of warships for action, and it was September 15 before Jefferson gave him notice of the request for his recall.[69] The long answer was a refusal to admit the power of the executive to bring about his dismissal. He was awaiting the assembling of Congress, he said, and until then he was finding solace for the perfidy of the administration in what " Veritas " and " Helvidius " were publishing in the newspapers.[70] Washington would have preferred to see the entire set of charges against Genêt published, to remove any suggestion of reference to Congress by convincing the people of the propriety of the government's measures.[71] But the only· purpose this would have served at this late date would have been to give a decision between " Helvidius " and " Pacificus " on the merits of their arguments in the press. Substantially all of the facts were already known to the public.

Reports of an expedition starting in Kentucky towards New Orleans, promoted by four Frenchmen whom Genêt had instructed, were followed up by advice to the Governor of the

---

[67] Writings, vol. viii, p. 14.
[68] Ibid., vol. viii, p. 31; Jefferson to Genêt, Oct. 3, to Morris, October 3, and to the President, October 3, 1793, all J. MSS.
[69] Writings, vol. viii, p. 46.
[70] Am. St. P., For. Rel., vol. i, p. 172.
[71] Washington to Jefferson, Oct. 7, 1793, Washington, Writings, vol. xii, p. 331.

State, Isaac Shelby. He was told to use force if the law was not sufficient to stop the movement, and General Knox was given that responsibility also. The news was carried to Jefferson in the first place by Viar and Jaudenes. They were kept informed of the safeguards, and were satisfied.[72] The expedition broke down because Genêt failed to furnish money for it.

As the time for the meeting of Congress drew near, Jefferson placed before Washington some materials for the message. The most important part of his contribution was that which called for the transformation of the basis of neutrality from an executive policy to legislative enactment. The message, December 3, incorporated his idea in a section, as follows:

> "It rests with the wisdom of Congress to correct, improve, or enforce, this plan of procedure; and it will probably be found expedient to extend the legal code and the jurisdiction of the courts of the United States to many cases which, though dependent on principles already recognized, demand some further provision." [73]

This was one of Jefferson's most significant contributions. The policy was directed, by his influence, from a temporizing expedient into a standard of conduct for the years to come. Almost as significant was his conquest of his own partizanship. The logic, the fairness, and the industry with which he followed up cases, whether French or British, and in spite of the difference of his feelings for the two nations, made Washington's peace plan a success. The very fact of Genêt's downfall is a tribute to Jefferson's support of the policy of neutrality. At the very end of his term he explained why he had insisted that the word "modern" should be used with "usage of nations" in the proclamation, designating it as a reference to the desirable rule that as to searches and seizures at sea, goods should follow the owner, and not the vessel. But the meaning of that word since his day, and because of his rulings, has come to have the actual meaning of "modern" in that sense of the "improvements which mark the advancement of civilization in modern times."

---

[72] Jefferson to Viar and Jaudenes, Nov. 6 and 10, 1793; to the Governor of Kentucky, Nov. 7, 1793, J. MSS.

[73] Am. St. P., For. Rel., vol. i, p. 39; Fenwick, p. 6.

BIBLIOGRAPHY

Manuscripts.

The Jefferson Papers. Library of Congress.
> These manuscripts have been the chief reliance for the study. Jefferson committed practically all of his thoughts to paper, either in the form of letters or as notes, and kept letter-press copies of his correspondence. Hence his papers are unusually complete. There are also original copies of letters to him from Lafayette, Monroe, Adams, Short, Carmichael, and a host of persons of lesser consequence. Of the two hundred and thirty-six volumes in which his papers are bound, those numbered from fourteen to ninety-six, containing about ten thousand enclosures, were used.

The Washington papers. Library of Congress.
> These were used for the period from 1790 to 1793. Several of the written reports of members of the Cabinet, as yet unprinted, are in these papers.

The Hamilton Papers. Library of Congress.
> Used for the same dates as the Washington Papers, and to supplement his printed works.

British State Papers, Hammond Correspondence.
> The Henry Adams transcripts in the Library of Congress. Used for a few of Hammond's reports to his home government.

Affaires Etrangères, Correspondance Politique, Etats-Unis.
> Also transcripts in the Library of Congress.

Printed Sources.

American State Papers, Foreign Relations, Lowrie and Clarke, Washington, 1832-1839.
> These consist of the papers that were laid before Congress. The originals of those with which Jefferson was connected are to be found in his papers.

Annals of Congress. Washington, 1834-1856.

Correspondence between Genêt and United States Officials, Washington, 1837.

Diplomatic Correspondence of the United States, 1783-1789. F. P. Blair, Washington, 1833-1834.

Ford, W. C., The United States and Spain in 1790. Washington, 1890.

Journals of the Continental Congress, 1774-1789. Hunt and Ford, Washington, 1904.

Journal of the Executive Proceedings of the Senate, Washington, 1820.

Treaties and Conventions concluded between the United States of America and other Powers. Washington, 1889.

Secret Journals of Congress, 1775-1788. Boston, 1821.

De Martens, Receuil des Principaux Traites. Paris, 1791.

Moore, J. B., Digest of International Law. Washington, 1906.

——, History and Digest of International Arbitration to which the United States has been a Party. Washington, 1898.

Reports of Committees relating to the Department of Foreign Affairs, No. 25 of the Papers of the Continental Congress.

Scott, J. B., Treaties between the United States and Prussia, N, Y., 1918.

——, The Armed Neutralities of 1780 and 1800. New York, 1918.

Turner, F. J., Correspondence of the French Ministers to the United States, 1791-1797. American Historical Association, Annual Reports, 1903.

Wharton, F., Diplomatic Correspondence of the American Revolution, Washington, 1889.

Printed Collections and Writings.

Adams, C. F., The Works of John Adams. Boston, 1850-1856.

Beard, C. A., Economic Origins of Jeffersonian Democracy. New York, 1915.

Bell, H. C., Trade Relations between the British West Indies and North America. English Hist. Review, July, 1916.

Bemis, S. F., Jay's Treaty. New York, 1923.

Beveridge, A. J., Life of John Marshall. New York, 1919.

Bowers, C. G., Jefferson and Hamilton. Boston, 1926.

Carpenter, S. C., Memoirs of Thomas Jefferson. 1809.

Chalmers, G., Opinions on Interesting Subjects of Public Law and Commercial Policy arising from American Independence. London, 1784.

Channing, E., History of the United States. New York, 1905-.

Corwin, E. S., French Policy and the American Alliance. Princeton, 1916.

De Witt, C., Jefferson and American Democracy. N. Y., 1866.

Dunbar, L. B., Monarchical Tendencies in the United States, 1776-1801. Urbana, 1923.

Dupuy, E., Americains et Barbaresques. Paris, 1920.

Fenwick, C. G, The Neutrality Laws of the United States, Washington, 1913.

Forman, S. E., Life and Writings of Thomas Jefferson, Indianapolis, 1904.

Goebel, J. L., The Recognition Policy of the United States. 1915.

Hazen, C. D., Contemporary American Opinion of the French Revolution. Baltimore, 1897.

Hill, C. E., Leading American Treaties. New York, 1922.

Hirst, F. W., Life and Letters of Thomas Jefferson, New York. 1926.

Hunt, G., History of the State Department. New Haven, 1914.

Jay, W., Life of John Jay. New York, 1837.

Johnston, R. H., Contribution to the Bibliography of Thomas Jefferson. Washington, 1905.

Lyman, T., Diplomacy of the United States. Boston, 1826.

McLaughlin, A. C., Western Posts and British Debts. Amer. Hist. Assoc., Annual Reports, 1894.

Mahan, A. T., Sea Power and its Relation to the War of 1812. Boston, 1905.

Marshall, J., Life of Washington, Philadelphia, 1804-1807.

Muzzey, D. S., Thomas Jefferson. New York, 1918.

Nussbaum, F. L., Commercial Policy in the French Revolution. Phila., 1923.

——, American Tobacco and French Politics. Pol. Sci. Quart., Dec., 1925.

Parton, J., Life of Thomas Jefferson. Boston, 1874.

——, Life and Times of Benjamin Franklin. Boston, 1867.

Phillips, P. C., The West in the Diplomacy of the American Revolution. Urbana, 1914.

Randall, H. S., Life of Thomas Jefferson. 1858.

Reeves, J., History of the Laws of Navigation. London, 1792.

Schouler, J., Thomas Jefferson. New York, 1919.

Trescott, W. H., Diplomatic History of the Administrations of Washington and Adams. Boston, 1851.

Tucker, G., Life of Thomas Jefferson. 1837.

Turner, F. J., Policy of France toward the Mississippi Valley. Amer. Hist. Review, X.

Williams, J. S., The Permanent Influence of Thomas Jefferson on American Institutions. New York, 1913.

Winsor, J., The Western Movement. New York, 1897.

Wood, G. C., Congressional Control of Foreign Relations during the American Revolution, 1774-1789. New York, 1917.

Woodbury, M., Public Opinion in Philadelphia, 1789-1801. Northampton, 1920.

Guides.

Calendar of the Correspondence of Thomas Jefferson. Bulletins Nos. 6, 8, and 10 of Bureau of Rolls and Library of the Department of State.

McLaughlin, A. C., Report on the Diplomatic Archives of the Department of State. Washington, 1906.

Van Tyne, C. H., and Leland, W. G., Guide to the Archives of the United States. Washington, 1907.

INDEX

Adams, John, on commercial treaty with England, 2; in Paris, 13; on Barbary relations, 28, 29; on Portuguese treaty, 68; in London, 85.

Algiers, captures of American vessels by, 23; Lamb's Mission to, 25-28; blockade of, proposed, 27, 29, 35, 38; American captives in, 31, 33, 35; tribute paid to, 37; failure of negotiation with, 38.

Alien rights, 10.

"Alliance," the, 58.

Alliance, French. See Treaties.

Anglomen, 99, 112.

Armed Neutrality of 1780, 4, 11.

Barbary States, 12, 20-39.

Barclay, Thomas, 20, 22-25, 36, 38, 58.

Bernis, Committee of, 45-47.

Blockade, 11.

Brazil, 71.

Calonne, 43, 45.

Carmichael, William, 23, 25, 28, 60, 72, 74, 82, 83.

Ceres, the, 13.

Commerce, report on, 92.

Commercial policy, 11, 43, 48, 52-56, 64, 85.

Commercial treaties. See Treaties.

Congress, committees on treaties, 3, 8-13; and Treaty of 1783, 5.

Consuls, contraband of war, 10, 65, 69; basis for authority, 60; arrest of, 61; negotiation of convention for, 62; exequators, 120.

Debts, British, 86, 96; French, 104.

Declaration of Independence, 44.

Denmark, 67.

Discriminatory duties, 87, 100.

Dumas, Charles, 19.

Extradition, 77.

Farmers-General, 15, 43, 51.

Fish. See Trade.

Florida Blanca, Count de, 23, 25.

Flour. See Trade.

Franklin, Benjamin, 4, 7, 12, 19.

"Free ships free goods," 11, 14.

Genêt, Citizen, 105, 111-120.

Hamilton, Alexander, against commercial war, 90; and Beckwith, 91; and Hammond, 94; on French treaties, 109.

Hammond, George, 91, 94, 108, 114.

Hartley, David, 2, 7, 14.

"Helvidius," 120.

Holy Roman Empire, 66.

Humphreys, Col. David, 36, 38, 70.

International law, property of sovereign, 59; consular immunity, 62-63; immunity aboard warships, 65; extradition, 79; navigation, 83; legitimacy, 104; alliances, 109; and Supreme Court of U. S., 116.

Jay, John, elected Secretary for Foreign Affairs, 8; on trade regulation, 16; on French trade, 49; on neutrality, 107.

Jefferson, Thomas, in Congress, 5, 8-13; views on commercial treaties, 7, 12, 15-18; minister plenipotentiary, 9; voyage to France, 13; report on Barbary, 34; responsibility in trade policy, 49; on freedom in trade, 52-56, 101; accused by Mirabeau, 56; service in creating consular convention, 65; on treaty with Portugal, 68; on diplomacy with Spain, 71, 75, 77, 82; on the "gen-

eral welfare " clause, 79; on
trade with England, 86, 90;
opposed to British conquests,
88; suspicions of Hamilton,
93, 119; answer to Hammond,
97; on Jay's Treaty, 99; on
foreign entanglements, 102;
on the policy of neutrality,
104-121; on French treaties,
109; on French prizes, 112; on
Genêt's recall, 118.
Jones, John Paul, 37, 67.

King, Rufus, 108.

Lafayette, Marquis de, 21, 42,
46, 99.
Lamb. John, 22, 25-28.
" Little Sarah," the, 116-118.
Livingston, Robert, 2.

Madison, James, 116.
Mahan, A. T., quoted, 1.
Mathurins, Order of, 30, 32.
Mississippi, navigation of, 80 ff.
Monopolies, French commercial,
15, 41, 45, 48, 52, 55.
Monroe, James, 14, 40, 84, 115.
Morocco, project for treaty with,
12, 22; captures of American
vessels, 21; Barclay's mission
to, 23-25; Treaty of 1787, 24.
Morris, Gouverneur, 88, 105.
Morris, Robert, 45.
Most favored nation principle,
14-18, 24, 101.
Moustier, Count de, instructions
to, 110.
Navigation Acts, English, effects
on United States trade in
West Indies, 3; renewal of,
1792, 96.
Neutrality, policy of, 99, 106;
proclamation, 107; legal basis
of, 115, 121.
Nootka Sound, 88.

O'Brien, Capt. Richard, 23, 33,
37.

Pagan's case, 93.
Passy, 13.
Pinckney, Thomas, 38.

Portugal. See Treaties.
Prizes, shelter for, 82; restora-
tion of French, 112, 114, 119.
Privateers, 14, 111.
Privy Council, 89.
Prussian Treaty, 14, 18.
" Publicus," 115.

Ransom, 26, 32, 35, 36.
Republicans, 118.
Rice. See Trade.

Short, William, 19.
Slaves, 91.
Spain, American possessions, 73;
and Creek Indians, 74-76; envoys in United States, 75.

Tobacco. See Trade.
Trade, West Indian, 3, 43, 49,
56, 87, 101; flour, 15, 56, 70;
tobacco, 16, 41, 45, 51, 96;
free, 18; Mediterranean, report on, 34; with France,
40 ff.; 105; whale oil, 42, 53-
56; fish, 44, 46; rice, 50.
Treaties, instructions for commercial, 9; proposed commercial, 14; most favored nation
principle in, 14-18; power of
Confederation in, 17; and
House of Representatives, 36;
as law, 44, 76; projected, with
Portugal, 68; instructions for
Spanish, 82; of alliance with
France, 99, 105, 108.
Treaty of 1783, ratification of,
5; non-execution of, 86, 95 ff.;
States actions on, 98.
Tribute, Barbary, 12, 26, 29, 32
35, 37.

Vergennes, Count de, 12, 21, 41,
99.

Washington, George, views on
Spain, 76, 81, 84; on French
treaties, 102; on neutrality,
103, 117.
West Indies. See Trade.
Western posts, 91.
Whale oil. See Trade.